# PREACHING AND PRACTICAL MINISTRY

Preaching and Its Partners
*A series edited by Paul Scott Wilson*


PREACHING AND PRACTICAL MINISTRY
*Ronald J. Allen*

# PREACHING AND PRACTICAL MINISTRY

## Ronald J. Allen

St. Louis, Missouri

© Copyright 2001 by Ronald J. Allen

All scripture quotations, unless otherwise indicated, are from the *New Revised Standard Version Bible*, copyright 1989, Division of Christian Education of the National Council of the Churches of Christ in the United States of America. Used by permission. All rights reserved.

Cover design: Michael A. Domínguez
Cover art: © 1998 Artville
Interior design: Wynn Younker
Art direction: Michael A. Domínguez

This book is printed on acid-free, recycled paper.

Visit Chalice Press on the World Wide Web at
www.chalicepress.com

10  9  8  7  6  5  4  3  2  1                              01  02  03

**Library of Congress Cataloging–in–Publication Data**

Allen, Ronald J. (Ronald James), 1949–
   Preaching and practical ministry / by Ronald J. Allen.
      p.    cm. – (Preaching and its partners)
   Includes bibliographical references.
   ISBN 0-8272-2972-0
   1. Preaching.  2. Pastoral theology.  I. Title.  II. Series.
BV4211.3 .A44  2001
251 – dc21                                                    00-011578

Printed in the United States of America

*For*
*Sabbath,*
*last daughter welcomed into our hearts,*
*whose name bespeaks*
*the great rest*
*that God promises for*
*this fevered world*

# CONTENTS

Acknowledgments      ix

Introduction      1

1. Preaching in the Life System of the Congregation      5

2. The Preacher as Teacher      29

3. The Preacher as Pastor      47

4. The Preacher as Administrator      71

5. The Preacher as Missionary      95

6. The Preacher as Spiritual Leader      119

Subject Index      145

# ACKNOWLEDGMENTS

I thank Linda McKiernan-Allen, my life partner, for helping create a household in which this project could come to birth at the present time. Next to the weekly Breaking of the Loaf, her life is the most regular existential evidence of divine *hesed* (God's steadfast love) in my world. I thank Paul Scott Wilson for the invitation to think afresh about the matters in this volume, and for his sage and good-natured counsel. I thank Jon L. Berquist, Academic Editor of Chalice Press, for patience and insight. Colleagues at Christian Theological Seminary have helped sharpen my thinking, especially E. Byron Anderson, Assistant Professor of Worship and Director of Sweeney Chapel, who read the entire manuscript with a critical eye. Because of limitations of space, I have not been able to pursue many points raised by Professor Anderson. I thank other colleagues both in Christian Theological Seminary and in the wider community of Christian witness who read chapters and sharpened my thinking: Dorothy Bass (Chapter 1), Inagrace Dieterrich (Chapter 5), Kay Bessler Northcutt (Chapter 6), Janet Parachin (Chapter 6), Priscilla Pope-Levison (Chapter 5), G. Lee Ramsey, Jr. (Chapter 3), Michael Smith (Chapter 5), Peter Steinke (Chapter 1). Where I have not followed the counsel of these gracious readers, I am at my own peril.

# INTRODUCTION

This book considers interplay between preaching and the academic disciplines that support certain aspects of ministry. These disciplines include Christian education, pastoral counseling, missiology, leadership, and spirituality.[1] What can pastors learn from Christian education and other pastoral disciplines that will enhance their preaching? What can other disciplines learn from preaching? How can other disciplines enhance their support of the preaching ministry?

Preaching has its deepest effect in a congregation when it draws its breath in positive connection with other things that happen in the Christian community. Conversely, the effect of preaching diminishes when the sermon has little relationship with other things that happen in the local church. This book commends ways that the preacher can integrate the sermon fully into the congregational life system, and thereby magnify the possibility for the sermon to affect the community.

This volume examines the place of preaching in the congregation from a systems perspective. Systems thinking assumes that a social group comprises various elements that inherently affect one another. These elements are formal, informal, and tacit. I turn to systems analysis to help understand ways in which the various parts of the

---

[1]Worship is another discipline relevant for preaching, but it will not be considered here. For worship, see E. Byron Anderson, e.g., "Form and Freedom: The Discipline of Worship," *Encounter* 60 (1999), 271–82, and *Preaching in the Context of Worship*, ed. David M. Greenhaw and Ronald J. Allen (St. Louis: Chalice Press, 2000).

congregational system work together to enhance or frustrate the congregation as a community of the gospel.

As indicated by the title *Preaching and Practical Ministry*, this book is interested in the relationship of preaching to other components of ministry in congregations. A generation ago, John Killinger began a similar project with a poem by Wallace Stevens.[2] In the poem, the speaker places a jar on a hill in Tennessee. The jar becomes the reference point for everything else in that region. Killinger sees preaching as such a reference point for ministry. William Willimon speaks similarly of preaching as the integrative center of the pastorate.[3]

I do not argue that preaching should always be *the* focal point of the ministerial vocation. However, given the competing demands of ministry in congregations today, pastors need a presiding perspective from which to organize their energy. Preaching is this aspect of ministry for many pastors.

Within this discussion, I nest the relationship between the preacher and Christian practice. Following Alisdair MacIntyre, Craig Dykstra, Dorothy Bass, and others, the church is recovering the notion of practice as referring to intentional things the Christian community does repeatedly to shape identity, understanding, and behavior.

Preaching is such a practice.[4] It is both affected by and affects other Christian practices. Preaching can enhance (or frustrate) Christian practices in the congregational system. Furthermore, preaching can help the community assess the extent to which a congregation is a community constituting a cluster of Christian practices. Not all habitual attitudes and behaviors in the church are Christian practice. Some persistent dispositions and actions work against the formation of Christian identity (e.g., a congregation may tacitly agree not to welcome new members into the circle of companionship). Preaching can help the congregation name qualities that deform Christian life and suggest their reform.

After an overview of preaching in the life system of the congregation (chapter 1), the volume is divided into chapters that focus on preaching in relationship to conventional categories of ministry–Christian education (chapter 2), pastoral care and counseling (chapter 3), administration (chapter 4), mission (chapter 5), and

---

[2]Wallace Stevens, "Anecdote of the Jar," in John R. Killinger, *The Centrality of Preaching in the Total Task of Ministry* (Waco, Tex.: Word Books, 1969), 15.

[3]William H. Willimon, *Integrative Preaching: The Pulpit at the Center*, Abingdon Preacher's Library (Nashville: Abingdon Press, 1981).

[4]The judgment that preaching is a practice is a change of perspective from one I articulated in *Interpreting the Gospel: An Introduction* (St. Louis: Chalice Press, 1998), 12.

spirituality (chapter 6). A systems understanding of the congregation helps us realize that these aspects of ministry do not take place in separate compartments. They influence one another. For instance, participating in mission beyond the congregation can become a significant experience of Christian education. Preparing a sermon can contribute to the spiritual life of the pastor.

In each chapter, I define the nature and purpose of that part of the congregational system. I trace aspects of the history of that area of congregational life that are salient to preaching, with an emphasis on pertinent Christian practices. I mention ways that preaching can help Christian practices enhance that component of ministry. Every chapter suggests ways in which the discipline can contribute to preaching. Each chapter also offers points at which preaching challenges that dimension of congregational life and the discipline. I identify practical guidelines for the use of this material in ministry. The chapters conclude with a summary of points for preaching that are drawn from the chapter, as well as a challenge from the preaching community to the discipline that is the focus of the chapter, and suggestions for further reading.

# 1

# PREACHING IN THE LIFE SYSTEM OF THE CONGREGATION

My father was a dentist in a small town in the Ozark Mountains in southern Missouri. He completed dental school and began to work in the depths of the Depression (1931). Many people were poor. He told me that, in the early years of his work, a patient came to him with a toothache. The patient could not pay in cash, but bartered a chicken for treatment. The decayed tooth caused severe pain. The patient also was limping because of a stiff, swollen knee.

My father extracted the tooth. A few days later, he met the patient on the street. The patient was walking freely. My father joked, "How many chickens did you give the physician to clear up your knee?" The patient replied, "Not a one. When you pulled my tooth, my knee got right." My father could not directly confirm a link between the extraction of the tooth and the restoration of the knee, but he commented that the parts of the human body are so wired together that the patient might be right.

Whether the extraction of the decayed tooth was connected to the recovery of the knee, I do not know. But the larger point is well taken: the human body is an integrated system. The parts affect one another, even when we are not aware of their interaction.

The relationship of the parts of the body is analogous to the church and the relationship of its various elements. Indeed, the apostle Paul speaks of the church as the "body of Christ."[1]

> For just as the body is one and has many members, and all the members of the body, though many, are one body, so it is with Christ...the body does not consist of one member but of many...If the whole body were an eye, where would the hearing be?...[because the parts are joined], if one member suffers, all suffer together with it; if one member is honored, all rejoice together with it. (1 Corinthians 12:12, 14, 17, 26)

The different members of the body have different gifts. All gifts must work in concert for the church to embody its purposes.

This chapter first turns to general systems theory for a basic framework to help understand the church as a body and, in later chapters, to help explore the relationship of preaching to the various tasks of ministry.[2] The chapter then considers ways in which the recently rediscovered notion of Christian practice can help the congregational life system form and express Christian witness in its formal, informal, and tacit dimensions.[3] Systems theory need not be daunting. This chapter shows that it offers the preacher a helpful perspective.

## What Is a System?

A system is "a set of interdependent units that interact with each other in order to perform a set of functions."[4] Systems come in many sizes. The universe itself is a macro-system of inter-related systems. The physical environment is a system in which the many different parts of nature affect one another. An atom is a micro-system.

---

[1]For understanding the notion of body as a figure for human community in antiquity, see Dale B. Martin, *The Corinthian Body* (New Haven: Yale University Press, 1995), 92–96.

[2]I work in a general way with systems theory and do not focus on the specific approach to systems analysis developed by Murray Bowen, *Family Therapy in Clinical Practice* (New York: J. Aronson Publishing Co., 1978), whose theory is influential in some clergy discussions of the congregation as a system. I draw on some analysts influenced by Bowen, but within a wider frame of systems thinking.

[3]Several key aspects of systems theory are congenial to process (relational) thought that is formative for my own worldview. See especially Alfred North Whitehead, *Process and Reality,* corrected ed., ed. David Ray Griffin and Donald W. Sherburne (New York: Free Press, 1978), 58–59, 286–88, 307–9, 332, and Catherine Keller, *From a Broken Web* (Boston: Beacon Press, 1986).

[4]Lawrence Lindley, "Social Ministry: Moving from Individuals to Systems," *Encounter* 61 (2000): 82.

A social system is one in which "the units are individuals or groups of individuals, and the interactions are the social interactions that comprise relationships."[5] Systems overlap with other systems, e.g., racial/ethnic groups, economic systems, nations, states, towns, neighborhoods, and households. A congregation is a social system whose function is to witness to the gospel of God amidst the other systems of the world.

Each system has its own characteristics, but within each system all things affect one another. For instance, an oil spill near a seashore disfigures the shoreline and kills animals. The human community responds with a wide range of activities: Some people change the plans they had made to vacation at that seashore; some people clean up the spill; others formulate governmental policies to make it less likely that such accidents will happen again; still others locate alternative sources of energy so that we will not have to transport oil in tankers across the ocean; and some are sad because the world economic system creates elaborate means to transport oil from one continent to another while people on both continents go hungry.

Relationship is the key concept of systems thinking.[6] The system is a whole and is not simply a collection of individual parts. An event in one part of the system prompts changes in other parts.

Systems thinkers often distinguish between linear and systemic understandings of cause and effect. Linear thinking posits a cause-and-effect relationship between cause A and effect B. A preacher, for instance, may think that great sermons on mission (cause) are the reason that the congregation engages in mission (effect).

Systemic understanding, by contrast, understands cause and effect as the multiple ways in which the various parts of the system mutually influence one another. For example, great sermons on mission may

---

[5]Ibid.

[6]The literature of systems thinking is vast. For practical introductions to the systems perspective, with attention to the church, the following are helpful: Thomas R. Hawkins, *The Learning Congregation: A New Vision of Leadership* (Louisville: Westminster John Knox Press, 1997); Ronald W. Richardson, *Creating a Healthier Church: Family Systems Theory, Leadership, and Congregational Life,* Creative Pastoral Care and Counseling Series (Minneapolis: Fortress Press, 1996); Peter L. Steinke, *Healthy Congregations: A Systems Approach* (Washington, D.C.: The Alban Institute, 1996); R. Paul Stevens and Phil Collins, *The Equipping Pastor: A Systems Approach to Congregational Leadership* (Washington, D.C.: The Alban Institute, 1993); Peter L. Steinke, *How Your Church Family Works: Understanding Congregations as Emotional Systems* (Washington, D.C.: The Alban Institute, 1993); Kenneth R. Mitchell, *Multiple Staff Ministries* (Philadelphia: The Westminster Press, 1988); Edwin Friedman, *From Generation to Generation: Family Process in Church and Synagogue* (New York: The Guilford Press, 1985); Mansell E. Pattison, *Pastor and Parish: A Systems Approach,* Creative Pastoral Care Series (Philadelphia: Fortress Press, 1977).

be part of the reason that the congregation is engaged in mission, but the congregation as a wider system comes into play. The persons who lead the congregation in mission are magnetic personalities. Many members were raised to think that their life responsibility includes helping others. Every quarter the older women's group dedicates a check for world mission. The youth group sponsors summer worktrips. Christian education includes periodic emphases on mission. Leaders of the congregation work in mission projects; a lot of church decisions are made informally while building houses. In official church meetings, leaders unconsciously lend more credence to the voices of those who have been on mission projects. Sermons contribute to the mission consciousness of the congregation, but are not solely responsible for the congregation's willingness to step beyond the edge of the church lawn. Indeed, a mission-minded congregation may help a preacher become more mission-oriented in weekly sermons.

Pastors often become interested in systemic thinking because it helps us deal with problems in the congregation. Systems thinkers stress that a problem in a church can almost never be understood by itself. A problem is almost always a function of the system. Consequently, dealing with the problem has system-wide consequences.

However, systems thinking should not await the appearance of a problem. Most congregations would profit from thinking systemically about the community when the system is functioning well. Such reflection would help them understand why the system is effectively serving its purpose and how they can tend its positive aspects.

## The Congregation as Life System

A congregation is not just any social system. It has a distinctive purpose.

> The church is the community of human beings called into existence by God, through the Holy Spirit, to live from and by the gospel of God. The church witnesses to the grace and command of the gospel as the call and claim of the God of Israel offered to the entire world, and hence to the church, through Jesus Christ. It does so both to remind itself of what it is about, and, on behalf of the world, that the world might one day reflect the glory of God. The church is both a recipient of the gospel and a sign of God's presence and purposes for the rest of the cosmic family.[7]

[7]Clark M. Williamson and Ronald J. Allen, *The Vital Church: Teaching, Worship, Community, Service* (St. Louis: Chalice Press, 1998), 25–26.

In short, the church is to embody the gospel in its own life, and is to witness to the gospel for the sake of other persons and systems.

The gospel is the news, confirmed to the church through Jesus Christ, of God's unconditional love for each and every created entity, and God's will for justice for each and every created entity.[8] The gospel is thus dipolar, containing both grace (the news of God's unconditional love) and command (the call of God for justice). The gospel is an ellipse–a circle with two centers. In this way of thinking, justice is right and loving relationship. The just world is one in which all persons, relationships, and situations embody God's purposes. God's will for justice is for all people, relationships, and circumstances to mediate God's love for each and all. The gospel is the center of the life of the church.

The church does not create itself, but is called into existence by God through the Holy Spirit. The Spirit is always present throughout the life system of the congregation. I do not mean that everything that happens in the congregation is the direct result of the leading of the Spirit. Sin is also present in the church. Elements in the congregational system can wittingly or unwittingly choose not to follow the Spirit. When that happens, God does not abandon the church. God works with the choices that the church makes to help the church manifest the light that it can, given the decisions it makes.

## Theological Criteria to Help the Church Reflect on Its Life System

In order to fulfill its mission, the congregation needs to understand its system as a whole, and the constituent parts, from the standpoint of the gospel. The congregation can then determine actions of change or reinforcement that are designed to help the community testify to the gospel throughout its life. Toward this end, the community can evaluate all aspects of its life by three criteria.[9]

### APPROPRIATENESS TO THE GOSPEL

The Christian community seeks to determine the degree to which every element of its life system is appropriate to the gospel. The community can apply this criterion to everything in its life world, such as every biblical text, Christian doctrine and practice, ethical action, personal and social situation, and every voice in the preaching conversation. "Is this element of the congregational system, and its

---

[8]Clark M. Williamson and Ronald J. Allen, *A Credible and Timely Word: Process Theology and Preaching* (St. Louis: Chalice Press, 1991), 71–90.

[9]For the derivation of these criteria, see ibid., 71–129.

attendant dynamics, appropriate to the news of God's unconditional love promised to each and all and God's call for justice?" The preacher seeks to identify the degree to which practices demonstrate or subvert the gospel.

An aspect of the life system may be altogether appropriate to the gospel. It may be ambiguous, that is, containing elements that are both appropriate to the gospel and inappropriate to the gospel. A part of the congregation's world may be altogether inappropriate to the gospel.

Four forms of subverting the gospel are especially common in Christian systems: works righteousness, cheap grace, denying that God loves all persons, and injustice. In works righteousness, an element of the community assumes that persons must perform works in order for God to love them. From this standpoint, we must earn God's love. The doctrine of justification by grace through faith asserts the opposite: we are justified by grace. Cheap grace occurs when we accept God's love for ourselves but do not respond by loving others with the love that God shows for us. For instance, a congregation may assure racists that God loves them without stressing that racism contradicts Christian identity and behavior. The congregational system can deny that God loves all people; some congregations exclude people formally and informally for arbitrary reasons. The system can also act unjustly toward some people and thereby participate in injustice. Many congregations, for example, use paper goods in ways that are environmentally damaging.

## INTELLIGIBILITY

The Christian community is called to a life that is intelligible in the contemporary world. This criterion has three components.

1. The claims of the Christian community must be *clear enough for people to understand them.* This component is informational and applies particularly to formal dimensions of the congregational system. The congregation needs to be able to get the point of the element. Systems sometimes malfunction because members of the community do not have basic information about the purposes of the system and its parts.

2. Each claim of the Christian community must be *logically consistent* within itself, and must be logically consistent with other things that the Christian community believes, says, and does. The church seeks a life system in which all elements

are logically consistent with God's love and call for justice. The purpose of this subcriterion is to help the pieces of the life system work in harmony with one another. When parts of the congregational world are inconsistent, they undercut one another, and they destroy the integrity of the system. The system can even deteriorate to the point that it works against its aim of witnessing to the gospel. Since a congregation represents God's relationship with the world, contradictions in the life system of the congregation can subtly raise the question of whether God has integrity and is trustworthy.

The preacher can commend witnesses that are logically consistent with the gospel. When voices in the preaching conversation are inconsistent with the gospel, the preacher can help the congregation understand the discrepancy between the gospel and the witnesses, and can help the community envision what to do and say to be consistent with the gospel.

3.  Each claim of the Christian community must be *believable.* In the pungent phrase of Yale theologian David Kelsey, it must be "seriously imaginable." Given the ways the contemporary community understands the world and its working, the congregational system and its parts must make sense.[10]

The church must handle carefully the notion of intelligibility. The church and the world must be able to accept the church's claims about God's presence, promises, and activity in the world as true within our interpretations of experience. The life system of a congregation pushes people toward unintelligibility and unbelievability when it urges the community members to disown what they otherwise observe to be true, or to embrace possibilities that contradict experience. Preaching themes that are not seriously imaginable destroys the credibility of Christian faith. However, the gospel may call the congregation to expand or revise its perception of the world and God's roles in it. The gospel can call us to realize that our understanding of God and the world are too limited.

The use of this criterion involves continual interpretation and reinterpretation of how the church understands the world. The plain

---

[10]David Kelsey, *Proving Doctrine: The Uses of Scripture in Modern Theology* (Harrisburg, Pa.: Trinity Press International, 1999, o.p. 1975), 170–74.

fact is that individuals and groups alter their perceptions of the cosmos as they come in contact with fresh perspectives and data. For example, quantum physics is now accepted as a better way of explaining the world than Newtonian physics. Is quantum physics the final word in these matters? We cannot say. Leading postmodern thinkers urge us to recognize that different human societies understand the world in different ways. The Earthwide human population does not subscribe to one worldview but to many. Consequently, the congregation needs to listen to other interpretations of the world to gauge the degree to which it might help the church move toward a more adequate understanding.

## Moral Plausibility

This criterion is derived from the norm of appropriateness, but focuses explicitly on the ethical treatment of all in the life system of the congregation, and in the world beyond the congregation. God's promise of unconditional love for each and all and God's insistence on justice for each and all carry with them a strong moral imperative. This criterion is distinctly practical. Any element of the life system of the congregation–a biblical text, a doctrine, a practice, formally authorized behavior, informally approved actions–can manifest attitudes that deny God's love or justice to some. Anti-Jewish elements of the Christian world, for instance, functionally communicate that God does not love the Jewish people and deny that God seeks justice for the Jewish community. A preacher is obliged to urge the congregation to say no to morally implausible elements in its life system. More than encouraging the congregation to say no, a preacher needs to help the congregation envision how the gospel can create a world in which all persons and elements of nature experience love and justice.

The preacher can apply these criteria to each element in the life of the community and to their system interaction. At what points do the element and the system enhance the gospel witness? Frustrate it? The congregation can then take steps to encourage qualities that enhance gospel witness and correct qualities that work against the gospel.

## Christian Practices and the Congregational Life System

A renewed notion of Christian practice helps us better understand how the life system of the congregation can help form and express Christian identity. Only a few years ago, many people considered practice to be someone doing something to achieve an immediate end, with little regard for traditions or communities associated with the activity.[11] For instance, my father, a dentist, spoke of his practice, that is, the patients whom he served and the things he did in their dental care.

About a decade ago, the church began to recover an older and more profound notion of practice fueled by the definition of Alisdair MacIntyre.

> By a "practice" I am going to mean any coherent and complex form of socially established co-operative human activity through which goods internal to that form of activity are realized in the course of trying to achieve those standards of excellence which are appropriate to, and partially definitive of, that form of activity, with the result that human powers to achieve excellence, and human conceptions of the ends and goods involved, are systematically extended.[12]

A practice is an endeavor of a particular community that has a particular history and its own body of knowledge.

My colleague E. Byron Anderson, drawing on MacIntyre and others, finds that a practice is an *intentional* activity, *repeated* over time, in order to *form* thoughts, feelings, and behaviors in community.[13] Practices take place in two related ways: (a) The community generates ritual actions that, in miniature, form the community in its understanding of the world. Placing an offering on the Lord's table is a practice that forms us in the notion that we are to offer our whole lives to God. (b) The community then lives out the ritual practices in the rest of its life. When I leave the sanctuary, I know that everything I do is supposed to be an offering to God. Ritual practices represent

---

[11]Craig Dykstra, "Reconceiving Practice," in *Shifting Boundaries: Contextual Approaches to the Structure of Theological Education,* ed. Barbara G. Wheeler and Edward Farley (Louisville: Westminster/John Knox Press, 1991), 35.

[12]Alisdair MacIntyre, *After Virtue,* 2d ed. (Notre Dame, Ind.: University of Notre Dame Press, 1984), 187.

[13]E. Byron Anderson, e.g., "Form and Freedom: The Discipline of Worship," *Encounter* 60 (1999): 271–82. For further work by E. Byron Anderson, see the following articles: "O For a Heart to Praise My God: Hymning the Self Before God," in *Liturgy and the Moral Self: Humanity at Full Stretch Before God,* ed. E. Byron Anderson and Bruce T. Morrill (Collegeville: The Liturgical Press, 1998), 111–26; "Table Etiquette and Kingdom Practice," *Encounter* 59 (1998): 77–93; "Liturgical Catechesis: Congregational Practice as Formation," *Religious Education* 92 (1997): 349–63; "Praying and Knowing," *Encounter* 57 (1996): 379–89; "Performance, Practice and Meaning in Christian Baptism," *Worship* 69 (1995): 482–504.

how we are to live in our wider worlds. Practice leads to "a way of life."[14] Practices of this kind have tremendous power to influence the life system of the congregation, often at deep, subliminal levels.

A congregation is a community of the practice of Christian faith. Craig Dykstra, a Christian educator and leader in this movement, points out, "Christian practices are things Christian people do together over time in response to and in the light of God's active presence for the life of the world."[15] The purpose of Christian practice is to impart Christian identity and to foster witness. Dykstra names thirteen such practices that constitute the heart of what it means to be a Christian community:

- Worshipping God as a community (praising, giving thanks, hearing the gospel interpreted through preaching, responding by offering ourselves in divine service, receiving the bread and the cup)

- Telling the Christian story to one another by reading and hearing the Bible and the story of the church through history

- Interpreting the Bible and the history of the church's experience so that we can understand the significance of these things for the contemporary world

- Praying both in corporate settings and individually

- Confessing sin to God and to one another, seeking forgiveness and reconciliation

---

[14]Craig Dykstra and Dorothy C. Bass, "Times of Yearning, Practices of Faith," in *Practicing our Faith: A Way of Life for a Searching People,* ed. Dorothy C. Bass (San Francisco: Jossey-Bass, 1997), 6. For other, representative works that illumine this direction, see Dorothy C. Bass, *Receiving the Day: Christian Practices for Opening the Gift of Time* (San Francisco: Jossey-Bass, 2000); Craig Dykstra, *Growing in the Life of Faith: Education and Christian Practices* (Louisville: Westminster /John Knox Press, 1999); Robert Wuthnow, *After Heaven: Spirituality in America since the 1950s* (Berkeley and Los Angeles: University of California Press, 1998), 168–98; Rebecca Chopp, *Saving Work: Feminist Practices of Theological Education* (Louisville: Westminster/John Knox Press, 1995), esp. 15–18; David Kelsey, *To Understand God Truly: What's Theological About a Theological School* (Louisville: Westminster/John Knox Press, 1992), 118–24; Susanne Johnson, *Christian Spiritual Formation in the Church and Classroom* (Nashville: Abingdon Press, 1989); Elaine Ramshaw, *Ritual and Pastoral Care,* Theology and Pastoral Care Series (Minneapolis: Fortress Press, 1987); Craig Dykstra, "The Formative Power of the Congregation," *Religious Education* 82 (1987): 530–47; id., "No Longer Strangers: The Church and Its Educational Ministry," *Princeton Seminary Bulletin* 6 (1985): 188–200.

[15]Dykstra and Bass, "Times of Yearning," 5.

- Tolerating one another in our failures and encouraging one another to conform more fully to the witness to which God calls us
- Carrying out acts of service and witness as a community
- Suffering with and for one another and for all with whom we are neighbors
- Providing hospitality and care for one another and for strangers–persons outside the Christian community
- Listening attentively so that we can understand one another and can know how to serve one another in the gospel
- Struggling together to interpret from the perspective of the gospel the many interlocking contexts in which our congregations live today
- Criticizing and resisting the principalities and powers that corrupt God's intentions for individual human lives, for human community, and for the world of nature
- Working together to maintain social structures that will sustain life as God intends[16]

These practices are essential to Christian community, but the list is not exhaustive. Many other aspects of congregational life can become practices when they are informed by theological vision and intentionally repeated to form Christian identity.

The practices derive from Christian tradition, communicate Christian perceptions of the world, and intend to bring forth Christian fruit in personal and communal life. They address basic human needs and circumstances by means of specific human actions. If we invest ourselves in them repeatedly, they have the power to shape us as individuals and as Christian communities. They can be measured by criteria that help the community know whether we are doing them well or badly.[17]

Although I have enumerated thirteen practices, they are all interrelated. While not drawing on systems theory per se, Dykstra and Dorothy Bass (a church historian), remind us that in Christian community, the practices "flow into one another, each one making a

---

[16]Dykstra, *Growing in the Life,* 27–28. Dykstra is not designated as the author of this list in *Growing in the Life of Christian Faith: A Way of Life for a Searching People* (San Francisco: Jossey-Bass, 1997) but is identified in Dorothy C. Bass, ed. *Practicing our Faith,* 205.

[17]Dykstra and Bass, "Times of Yearning," 6–8.

space for God's active presence that then ripple out into other parts of life."[18] Focusing on one practice inevitably leads to other practices.

The notion of practice is important in two ways. First, Christian faith is a way of life. We Christians are to engage in the practices wherever we are. In daily existence, we are to manifest the practices all the time. Second, the corporate acts of the gathered Christian community should enable us to learn the practices by engaging in them. The formal activities of the congregation give the congregation a chance to practice the practices in the same way that a child practices catching a ball or playing scales. In prayer group on Wednesday night, for instance, we not only pray for the world, for one another, and for ourselves, we also learn how to pray by praying in Christian community. The goal of the practices at both levels is to come to perceive how our daily lives are "all tangled up with the things God is doing in the world."[19]

These practices do not correlate in a one-to-one way with the organizational structure of the congregational life system. They are things that Christians do within the formal, informal, and tacit realms of the life system in order to form, deepen, or express Christian life orientation.

The practices provide specific Christian content to the formal things that happen in the congregation. The formal practices of worship, for instance, pattern the community to recognize and respond to God's presence. When the community leaves the sanctuary, it transfers the practices of worship to other settings in life. A member of our congregation in Nebraska once told me about a tearful chance encounter with another member near the dairy case of the supermarket late at night that became an occasion of confession of sin.

### Preaching as Practice

Although preaching does not appear by itself on the list of the thirteen practices, it is a part of worship and functions as a practice as an intentional activity repeated over time in order to form Christian identity, community, and witness. Thomas Hoyt, Jr., places preaching in the larger Christian practice of giving testimony. Testimony is the act of speaking truth as we have seen, heard, and experienced it. Testimony is a communal event. "The practice of testimony requires

---

[18]Ibid., 10.
[19]Ibid., 8.

that there be witnesses to testify and others to receive and evaluate their testimony."[20] The preacher does not speak imperially. In the spirit of 1 John 4:1, the community is to test the preacher's words "to see whether they are from God." Christian practice should develop the capacity for theological discernment in the community.

Testimony takes many forms in Christian community. The sermon is an instance of testimony in which the preacher speaks on behalf of the community by testifying to what the community sees, hears, and experiences. The preacher interprets the situations of the congregation and of the larger world from the perspective of the gospel. The sermon is an exemplary instance in that it demonstrates in the setting of worship the practice of giving testimony that is to be a part of the everyday lives of the members of the community.[21] When the people leave public worship, they should be able to interpret their immediate worlds and the larger world from the standpoint of the gospel.

When the practices in a congregation are faithful to the gospel, the practice of the practices should help the preacher articulate a distinctly Christian vision. The practices should help the congregation form a distinctly Christian set of mind and heart and will with which to receive the sermon. The theological content of the practices provides norms by which to evaluate the health of the congregation as a Christian life system.

## *Not All Repeated Activities in a Congregation Are Christian Practices*

Not all repeated activities in a congregation are Christian. Congregations can engage in habits of thought and feeling that purvey non-Christian, even anti-Christian, elements. For example, the church is called to practice hospitality for one another and for strangers. Some congregations practice hospitality toward one another, but tacitly shut out people who are new to the congregation. The latter behavior subverts the church. The practice (hospitality) becomes twisted by sin.

The leadership in the congregation is called to appraise the actual formal, informal, and tacit attitudes and behaviors in the congregation

---

[20]Thomas Hoyt, Jr., "Testimony," in Bass, *Practicing our Faith,* 92. For further discussion of testimony, see Rebecca Chopp, *The Power to Speak* (New York: Crossroad 1989), 59–66; id., "Bearing Witness: Traditional Faith in Contemporary Expression," *Quarterly Review* 17 (1997): 193–206; id., "Theology and the Poetics of Testimony," *Criterion* 37/1 (1998): 2–13.

[21]I thank Dorothy Bass for the notion of preaching as an exemplary instance of testimony. Personal correspondence.

for the degree to which they help shape genuinely *Christian* community. When a congregation discovers that it is actually working against the gospel, practices themselves provide a way to remedy the situation: confessing sin and tolerating one another in failure even while encouraging one another to conform more fully to God's purposes.

## Preaching in the Congregational System

Preaching is interpreting the significance of the gospel for the situation of the congregation and the world.[22] This theological interpretation takes place through conversation with the Bible, church history and doctrine, contemporary systematic theology, the physical and social sciences, the arts, and, especially, with members of the congregation. The preacher listens to these various voices and brings them into conversation to help the Christian community identify what God's unconditional love offers the life system of the congregation and the larger world, and what God's call for justice requires of the system and the world.[23]

Preaching intends to help the congregation reflect theologically on its life system—on both the interior dimensions of the congregation and on its relationship with the world beyond itself—so that the congregation can form and express itself as a community of the gospel.[24] To adapt a striking expression from Notre Dame theologian Mary Catherine Hilkert, the preacher helps the church *name* God's grace and its effects and requirements in the world of the congregation.[25]

By the way, I do not use the term *conversation* to suggest that the sermon should be a give-and-take out loud between the preacher and the congregation. Rather, I use conversation to suggest that the sermon, even when monological in form, should have the quality of a conversation in which the congregation joins the preacher in exploring the significance of the gospel for the circumstances of the community. A sermon can be monological in form but dialogical in character.[26]

---

[22]Allen, *Interpreting the Gospel,* 65–81.

[23]I suggest a twenty-seven-step model for sermon preparation in *Interpreting the Gospel,* 119–76.

[24]Cf. Ronald J. Allen, "Preaching in the Congregational System," *Encounter* 60 (1999): 551–82.

[25]Mary Catherine Hilkert, *Naming Grace: Preaching and the Sacramental Imagination* (New York: Crossroad, 1997).

[26]Allen, *Interpreting the Gospel,* 65–80.

From the perspective of systems theory, the sermon does not bear the sole responsibility for the vocation of the church. Every aspect of the life of the community can help (or frustrate) that vocation. A community often benefits from consideration of an issue when the issue is addressed in multiple parts of the congregation system. A preacher should regularly ask, "How can various parts of the congregational system work together on this issue?" For instance, a congregation's opportunities to interact with an issue are multiplied when it is considered in the sermon, in administrative deliberations, and in mission beyond the congregation.

As noted earlier, the preacher and the ways in which the preacher conceives the sermon are influenced by the congregation. The preacher is not a lone agent. Indeed, Craig Dykstra criticizes the image of the minister practicing the practices individually.[27] The preacher is always enmeshed in community. Dorothy Bass points out, "The sermon belongs to the whole body and exists in the hearing as well as in the proclaiming."[28] The state of practices in the congregation can create an ethos that shapes the preacher and the sermon. For example, a community that is alive to scripture because of its practice of interpreting the Bible may call the preacher to engage the Bible with fresh penetration.

The congregation sets the preacher aside through ordination to make sure that issues are considered in theologically adequate ways that honor tradition and that account for the full range of dynamics in the community.[29] Other leaders and groups in the congregation may perform this function, but the church designates the preacher to see that it happens.

Since the sermon takes place in worship–the most well-attended of the congregation's regular events–the sermon is a remarkable opportunity to introduce an issue into the system, or to bring an issue into the public arena of discussion. Indeed, an important purpose of preaching is to bring voices into congregational consciousness and conversation that are often overlooked, or even silenced.[30]

Preaching can help the community name the presence of the issue and begin to interpret it theologically. Along the way, the sermon

---

[27]Dykstra, "Reconceiving Practice," 42 ("practice is inherently *cooperative*"), 54–56.

[28]Dorothy Bass, personal correspondence.

[29]I do not mean to suggest that the preacher has a monopoly on theological insight. Because preachers are finite, we can make mistakes.

[30]On the importance of retrieving voices that have been unintentionally or intentionally omitted from the conversation, see Mary Donovan Turner and Mary Lin Hudson, *Saved from Silence: Finding Women's Voice in Preaching* (St. Louis: Chalice Press, 1999).

may draw on particular Christian practices to help the congregation remember things that it has forgotten or never known (e.g., passages from the Bible, doctrines, ethical expectations). A message can often help the congregation as a whole reframe its perception of an issue.

The sermon is also an opportunity to touch the system at a maximum number of places in a single moment, including a community-wide conversation and action outside the sanctuary. Because it reaches so many people, a sermon has a remarkable opportunity to help shape *how* the community approaches an issue. A sermon in a positive, sensitive, exploratory tone can often help a congregation be receptive to dealing with aspects of its system, whereas a negative, rigid, authoritarian tone can undermine the congregation's interaction. The experience of hearing the sermon creates a shared memory. This memory can be a vital resource as the congregation thinks, feels, and behaves its way into an issue.

A sermon need not always resolve the issue being discussed. In fact, if a preacher introduces a solution too quickly or in a manner that grates against congregational process, the preacher's suggestion may get lost. Systems thinkers point out that conflict can sometimes be an occasion for growth in the community. Frequently the community itself needs to work out the solution, using the sermon as valuable input.

Every sermon released in the system affects the community. Many sermons celebrate God's presence, and call the congregation to join the celebration. Some sermons are medicines that heal and are designed to ease pain. Other sermons are toxins, such as chemotherapy, that heal by destroying unhealthy parts of the body. Still other sermons are scalpels meant to open the body for purposes of healing.

A sermon may generate ripples that the preacher intends. However, a preacher cannot always predict how a sermon will affect the congregational system. When a sermon is released into the system, the effects are sometimes altogether unforeseen. Consequently, ministers need feedback on their preaching. Indeed, a sermon may become a part of a life process in the congregation that calls forth another sermon. The ripples caused by a sermon may change the ecosystem of the congregation such that they become ripples that cause other sermons. Ripples generated by other parts of the congregational system should affect a preacher's consciousness of the direction of the sermon.

Some sermons arise because the preacher begins with a biblical text and moves from that text to its implications for the congregational system and the wider world. Other sermons originate because the preacher becomes aware of an aspect of the congregational life system or the relationship of the congregation with the wider world that needs to be interpreted from the perspective of the gospel. A preacher should regularly ask, "Are issues surfacing in the congregation that the sermon can profitably address?" Whether beginning from a text or from a situation in the congregation, the preacher can often help increase the effect of the sermon (and minimize damage) by anticipating how the sermon might affect different parts of the congregation.

## Preaching and Formal, Informal, and Tacit Parts of the Congregational System

A system contains formal parts, informal parts, and tacit parts.[31] Some of these parts are the result of conscious, critical decisions on the part of members of the system. Other aspects of a system are more informal, emotional, and intuitive. Preaching has a reciprocal relationship with all these elements. They help shape the congregation's receptivity toward the sermon. At the same time, the sermon helps shape how these three elements function in the life system of the congregation

### *Formal Elements of the System*

The formal parts of a congregational system are usually authorized in writing or by a public agreement. They include things such as denominational affiliation and tradition (e.g., doctrine, polity), statements of beliefs, incorporation according to the laws of the state, a mission statement approved by the membership, the official organization of the congregation. In the congregational system, particular bodies are often formally responsible for specific aspects of congregational life.

Many denominations and theological movements have formal understandings of the function of the sermon.[32] In the Reformed tradition, for instance, the sermon teaches Christian faith and leads the congregation into an encounter with the living God. In the Orthodox churches, the sermon is a spoken icon through which the divine presence becomes visible in the community. These notions help preachers understand the role of the sermon in the Christian community.

---

[31]George Parsons and Speed B. Leas, *Understanding Your Congregation as a System* (Washington, D.C.: The Alban Institute, 1993), 9.
[32]Cf. Allen, *Interpreting the Gospel,* 24–28, 73–81.

Formal statements can serve as norms by which the preacher can evaluate all aspects of a system's life–formal, informal, and tacit. However, the formal dimensions of a system are not always the most life-shaping components within a system. Informal and tacit dimensions are frequently as important as formal ones, sometimes more so.

The preacher is called to help the community reflect on the degree to which the formal parts of the congregational life system function coherently with the purpose of Christian community. For instance, the preacher can help the congregation consider experiences of mission that take place beyond the congregation. Is such mission taking place? Who is involved? Do more people and resources need to be involved? How do the congregation's efforts at mission relate to the rest of the congregational system? Should adjustments be made in the system to help support mission beyond the congregation?

## *Informal Elements of the System*

As the name implies, the informal parts of a system function because of informal acknowledgments or roles among the members of the community. The acknowledgment is usually spoken, but is not a part of an official line of responsibility.

Informal relationships in a system can be quite powerful. For example, in the congregation in which I grew up, one of the informal responsibilities of the youth group sponsors was to take the youth group, after Sunday night worship, to the Blakeney Dairy Ice Cream Shop across the street from the church building. Although informal, those weekly trips were as important a ritual in our youth group as Bible school and worship on Sunday morning and youth meeting before worship on Sunday evening.

Informal elements can support a congregation's purpose. Sometimes, though, informal elements work against the formal purposes of the system and its lines of responsibility. For instance, a congregation contains a formal procedure for monitoring the relationship between congregation and pastor. However, a group of people in the congregation becomes unhappy with a pastor. These folk feed one another's frustrations at the local swimming pool. Without consulting the official channels, an informal leader of the group visits the pastor with news of this unhappiness. The pastor resigns. Others in the congregation feel betrayed by the informal group, and even by the pastor, who does not activate official grievance mechanisms.

The sermon can help the community reflect on the relationship between the actual behavior among the informal parts of the system and the purpose of the congregation. The sermon can name informal elements of the community and ask, "Are these aspects of our common life coherent with God's unconditional love for all and God's will for justice for all? What needs to happen in our community to reinforce gospel patterns, or to help change ways of relating that frustrate the church's being a community of the gospel?"

## *Tacit Elements of the System*

Tacit parts of the system are agreements and roles that are not acknowledged by speech. The tacit parts of the community consist of patterns or habits of thinking, feeling, and behaving that emerge in the group. People can be conscious of them, but they can also exist unconsciously within a group. An example of a tacit function is the assumption that a certain seat in the sanctuary belongs to a certain person.

Tacit dimensions can either serve or frustrate the purposes of the congregation. For instance, the mission statement of a congregation interprets the great commission of Jesus to "go and make disciples of all nations" (Matthew 28:16–20) to mean that the church is to invite persons who are not Christian to understand that God loves them unconditionally and, in response, these people are to affiliate with the church. The informal understanding of the congregation may be, "We need some new members." However, the tacit assumption of the core leadership may be, "Let's grow old together."[33] The members of the community do not really want to add new members.

Peter Steinke, a systems analyst who describes the congregation as an emotional system, points out that anxiety is one of the most pervasive emotions in the congregational system.[34] Anxiety is often activated by uncertainty. For example, threat of loss often triggers anxiety. Anxiety plays a mixed role in the congregational system. On the one hand, anxiety can "be our deliverance. It has motivational power. Anxiety provokes change."[35] On the other hand, when anxiety "reaches a certain intensity, it prevents the very change it seeks to provoke. What is stimulus becomes restraint. We 'lose our head,' or 'cool,' as we say…we are too reactive to be responsive."[36] Anxiety should be named and considered pastorally.[37]

---

[33]Parsons and Leas, *Understanding Your Congregation as a System,* 10.

[34]Steinke, *How Your Church Family Works,* x–xi, 13–25.

[35]Ibid., 14.

[36]Ibid., 14.

[37]Edwin Friedman calls for the pastor to be a "non-anxious presence," that is, pastors need to name their anxiety and contain it with respect to congregational matters. See his *From Generation to Generation,* 208–10.

The preacher needs to help the congregation name and reflect on the degree to which tacit factors in a congregation serve the gospel and the purpose of the church. As in the case of informal elements in the congregation, the sermon can ask, "Do the tacit dimensions of our common life work with other aspects of the system in ways that are consistent with the divine promise of unconditional love for each and all and the divine call for justice for each and all?" Of course, the minister must not violate confidentiality or place particular people in an awkward relationship with the congregation.

## Preaching and Christian Practices in the Congregation

Christian practices should function in every phase of the congregation. They should be a regular part of the formal life of the system because they are intentional and are to be repeated. Their occurrence in the formal settings of worship and Christian education can help them take root and appear elsewhere in the congregation.

They can also be a part of the community's informal and tacit worlds. Christian practices can help maintain a healthy system. For instance, in a congregation in which people understand themselves in terms of the gospel, telling the Christian story can be a means of reaffirming Christian identity in the face of persistent challenges to that identity from the larger environment. Christian practices can also help unbalance a system that is maintaining dysfunctional patterns and that needs to change. For example, criticizing and resisting the principalities and powers may bring the congregation to recognize that they collude with the principalities and powers that they are criticizing.

Worship is a particularly important practice for the preacher because the sermon takes life in the context of worship. In the service of worship, we use everyday things–food, water, oil, embrace, speech, singing–to announce and bless the redemptive presence and activity of God in the world. The service of worship represents the Christian life in the form of ritual words and actions. These actions are miniature enactments in the confined space of worship that symbolize what we are to do in the whole of life. In worship, the Christian congregation rehearses its way of life in the world. In worship we "practice the practices," in the same way that a child practices the scales or practices catching a ball, so that we can carry them out when we are in the symphony or in the game. Through the actions of worship, we acknowledge that existence is a gift from the Great Creator. We confess our failure to handle this gift as God intends. We hear stories from the Bible and from Christian tradition, and we speak words that interpret our lives in God's light. We receive assurance of divine grace, and offer ourselves to its service. We are sent out strengthened to live more fully in God's ways.[38]

The sermon can help the community hear the stories and speak words that relate our practices to God's own creative and redemptive work. The sermon helps the congregation to understand and experience the Christian practices as life shaping. The preacher helps the congregation remember the practices, and sparks the community to make the practices happen. The preacher explains particular Christian practices—their origins, their continuing significance, and their benefits. From time to time, the sermon should explain how to carry out some of the practices. Craig Dykstra puts the preacher's task succinctly. The preacher is to help the community recognize "the inner workings and qualities of each practice" so that those "workings and qualities open up to the reality and truth on which they are founded."[39]

Most of the time, a biblical text will provide the preacher with an opportunity to move from the text to a practice. However, ministers can preach directly on the practices themselves. For instance, a preacher could prepare a sermon on the practice of working together to maintain social structures that will sustain life as God intends. A pastor could turn to a topical sermon in which the practice itself is the basis of the sermon, much like a biblical text is the basis of an expository sermon.

In order for the congregation to fulfill its purpose in an optimum way, each element of congregational life must function effectively, and the various elements must work together in the service of the gospel. In such a situation, the different aspects of community life support one another.

## Implications for Preachers

The preacher is broadly called to interpret the life of the congregation and the life of the broader world from the perspective of the gospel. More specifically, from the standpoint of this chapter, the preacher is called to interpret the congregation as a life system intended to be shaped by Christian practice. Toward this end, the preacher has several distinct opportunities and responsibilities:

---

[38]Dykstra and Bass, "Times of Yearning," 9.
[39]Dykstra, "Reconceiving Practice," 54–55.

- Help the congregation understand its life as a system
- Reflect with the congregation on the system and its constituent parts from the perspective of the criteria of appropriateness to the gospel, intelligibility, and moral plausibility
- Take account of ways that the congregational system can (and should) affect the content of sermons (e.g., a fractious congregation might led the preacher to sermons on forgiveness)
- Identify ways that the sermon can work with other elements in the congregational system to strengthen the community's witness to the gospel
- Help the congregation to recognize and understand Christian practices (e.g., interpreting the Bible) and how they form Christian identity, attitudes, and actions
- Guide the Christian community in enhancing Christian practice by providing information on the history of the practices and on their contemporary enactment
- Use the criteria of appropriateness to the gospel, intelligibility, and moral plausibility to measure the testimony that is articulated in the sermon
- Help the congregation name and reflect theologically on the formal aspects of congregational life, and in a move that would be new to some preachers, also reflect on informal and tacit aspects
- Help the congregation recognize how its life system interacts (and should interact) with larger life systems in the world

## Implications for the Theory of Christian Practice

While this book is concerned broadly with the place of preaching in the congregational system, it does not approach the subject from a highly developed systems perspective. For that, preachers need books and articles that are more attuned to the nuances of systems theory.

For its part, preaching reminds pastors and authors who seek to understand the congregation in systems perspective to maintain a thoroughgoing theological framework. Systems thinkers are sometimes so absorbed by systems theory, and its attendant sociological and psychological insights, that these disciplines furnish the norms by which systems analysts gauge the life of a congregation. Such thinkers can lose sight of the fact that systems insights and their sociological and psychological components are supposed to be in the service of helping the congregation develop as a community of the gospel whose goal is to make a gospel witness.

Preachers also need books and articles that explore preaching as a Christian practice and the relationship of preaching to other Christian practices. Although preaching is among the practices that touches the largest numbers of members of the congregation at a single setting, it has not drawn sustained specific attention of leaders in the recovery of Christian practice. As I write, I know of only one book in preparation on preaching as a Christian practice.

## Suggestions for Further Reading

Ammerman, Nancy T., Jackson W. Carroll, Carl S. Dudley, and William McKinney, eds. *Studying Congregations: A New Handbook.* Nashville: Abingdon Press, 1998. Provides practical guidance for understanding the internal life of a congregation and the congregation's relationship to its larger worlds.

Bass, Dorothy C., ed. *Practicing our Faith: A Way of Life for a Searching People.* San Francisco: Jossey-Bass, 1997. A basic guide to Christian practices in the congregation.

Friedman, Edwin. *From Generation to Generation: Family Process in Church and Synagogue.* New York: The Guilford Press, 1985. Applies family systems theory to congregational life.

Steinke, Peter. *Healthy Congregations: A Systems Approach.* Washington, D.C.: The Alban Institute, 1996. Introduction to systems theory and the congregation.

# 2

# THE PREACHER AS TEACHER

How can preaching relate to Bible school classes so that sermon and classroom can work together in helping the community live toward fullness of Christian life? The question is a good one. However, it presupposes that Christian education is a *program*. Fresh thinking in the field of Christian education now regards Christian education as a function of the total congregational life system.

In this chapter, I recall how education was understood in Israel and the early Christian community. I then trace how the North American church has thought of Christian education as a program within the congregation. The heart of the chapter indicates an important shift taking place: we are now thinking of Christian education less as a program and more as a result of Christian practice throughout the congregation. I highlight the roles that preaching can play in Christian formation.

## From Israel through the Reformation: Church as Life System of Teaching

The biblical communities did not think in categories of contemporary systems perspective nor of community practice. Nonetheless, there are similarities between ancient and new emphases: people of antiquity regarded faith formation as taking place throughout community practice. Contemporary theory recovers this ancient thinking.

Israel and the church regarded themselves as communities of learning and teaching.[1] James Crenshaw, a major interpreter of the First Testament, finds that most teaching in Israel took place in the home, but was supported by schools, especially in the Hellenistic era (roughly 300 B.C.E. to 200 C.E.).[2] According to the Deuteronomic Moses, all that happens in the community is to help the community fulfill its identity as witness to God.

> Hear, O Israel: The LORD is our God, the LORD alone. You shall love the LORD your God with all your heart, and with all your soul, and with all your might. Keep these words that I am commanding you today in your heart. Recite them to your children and talk about them when you are at home and when you are away, when you lie down and when you rise. Bind them as a sign on your hand, fix them as an emblem on your forehead, and write them on the doorposts of your house and on your gates." (Deuteronomy 6:4–9)

The close relationship between preaching and education is indicated by the fact that the book of Deuteronomy is essentially an extended sermon on the part of Moses.

According to the priestly theologians, God is the great teacher (Isaiah 2:3). Meanwhile, God provides the community with instructors, including priestly teachers (Isaiah 50:4; Ezekiel 44:23). When the people do not know God, disobedience occurs and is followed by national collapse (e.g., Jeremiah).

The wisdom literature is permeated by concern for instruction. According to the sages, the goal of life is to gain wisdom, that is, the capacity to recognize God's purposes and to respond accordingly. Folly is the inability to recognize divine purposes. Many scholars think the term *sage* (wise person) referred to a teacher in the community. Community members also gain wisdom by observing nature and by reflecting on life.

The gospel writers repeatedly picture Jesus teaching. He is often called "Teacher" (*Rabbi*). A rabbi interprets the significance of the sacred traditions of Israel for the present. In the synoptic gospels, Jesus teaches the reign of God–the time when every relationship will

---

[1]Clark M. Williamson and Ronald J. Allen, *The Teaching Minister* (Louisville: Westminster/John Knox Press, 1991), 26–46, and Ronald J. Allen, *The Teaching Sermon* (Nashville: Abingdon Press, 1995), 13–16.

[2]James L. Crenshaw, "Education in Ancient Israel," *Journal of Biblical Literature* 104 (1985): 601–5; id., *Education in Ancient Israel: Across the Deadening Silence,* The Anchor Bible Reference Library (Garden City: Doubleday, 1998).

be as God intends. In the Fourth Gospel, Jesus instructs the disciples in the revelation of God.

The most frequent designation of Jesus' followers, *disciple*, is from the word family whose meaning is "to learn." The disciple learned the pattern of the teacher by living with the teacher, as well as through formal instruction. The process of making disciples involves the whole life system.

The early church moved in the tradition of Israel and the church. Luke's memory of the early Christian community is that they "devoted themselves to the apostles' teaching" (Acts 2:42). The first churches designated the function of teacher for the purpose of helping the community learn, remember, and interpret the importance of the traditions of Israel and the church (e.g., 1 Corinthians 12:28–29; Romans 12:7; Ephesians 4:11). Paul taught the ways of Christ everywhere so that believers could know and serve the God of Israel (1 Corinthians 4:17). False teaching became a problem in some communities (e.g., 2 Peter 2:1–3; 1 Timothy 1:10; 4:7; 6:3). Ephesians summarizes the goal of Christian teaching: to "equip the saints for the work of ministry, for building up the body of Christ, until all of us come to the unity of the faith and of the knowledge of the Son of God, to maturity, to the measure of the full stature of Christ" (Ephesians 4:12–13).

Education in Israel and the church sought to help the community discover God's offers and requirements. While Israel and the church established teaching offices, the communities typically followed the Deuteronomic theologians in thinking that faith formation should take place not only in a formal educational setting, but also in the home and throughout community life. We are rediscovering these themes in our day.

These emphases continued in the history of the church through the Reformation. The church became a system of faith formation through Christian practice, though prior to the medieval period, the church used catechetical schools (offering instruction in Bible and doctrine) to prepare persons for baptism. Participating in the home and congregation provided postbaptismal education.[3]

In the medieval period in Europe (from roughly the end of the fifth century through the fifteenth century), church and culture intertwined. Christendom emerged. Infants were baptized into the church, and children learned Christian identity and behavior by

---

[3]Marianne Sawicki, *The Gospel in History: Portrait of a Teaching Church, The Origins of Christian Education* (New York: Paulist Press, 1988), 110–44, esp. 125–39.

participating in Christian community. Formal programs of instruction diminished, though the church generated popular handbooks of Christian thought and appointed godparents to impart essentials of Christian faith to children. Monasteries nurtured Christian faith through daily practice. Preaching became a primary means for the congregation to encounter the Bible, doctrine, and ethics. [4]

The reformers renewed formal programs of Christian formation while continuing to stress the home and community practice. Close identification between church and culture made it easy for ecclesiastics to take a lead in developing schools that taught Christian faith alongside reading, mathematics, and other subjects. Several of the reform movements created catechisms for use in such schools. The reformers viewed the home as a Christian school. Geneva became a city in which every phase of life was supposed to teach Christian practice. Indeed, John Knox declared that Geneva was "the greatest school of Christ on earth."[5] In all phases of the reformation, the sermon was elevated to a moment of teaching par excellence.

## A Functionalist Approach

The industrial revolution spawned conditions in Europe and the United States that led to the most influential instrument of Christian education in the last two hundred years–the Sunday school. In Europe people flooded into cities to work in factories. The educational patterns that developed during the Reformation broke down, especially in urban areas. Households in the middle and upper classes sent their children to private schools. Many people in poverty lost contact with both the church and conventional education.

The Sunday school was born in the industrial slums of England with a dual mission: to provide basic education (in reading, writing, mathematics) and to offer basic Christian knowledge. Children worked in mines and factories through the week. On Sundays, they went to school. During the early years of this period, the sermon continued to be the leading mode of Christian education for adults.

The cultural situation was different in the United States, but the Sunday school still emerged as a vibrant force. By the early nineteenth century in the U.S., free public education was widespread. However,

---

[4]Milton McCormick Gatch, "Basic Christian Education from the Decline of Catechesis to the Rise of the Catechisms," in *A Faithful Church: Issues in the History of Catechesis,* ed. John H. Westerhoff III and O. C. Edwards, Jr. (Wilton, Conn.: Morehouse-Barlow, 1981), 79–108.

[5]Quoted in Wilhelm Pauck, "The Ministry in the Time of the Continental Reformation," in *The Ministry in Historical Perspectives,* ed. H. Richard Niebuhr and Daniel D. Williams (New York: Harper, 1956), 130.

religious education was seldom taught as a subject area in the public schools. Consequently, the Sunday school became the church's main vehicle of Christian education, gradually supplemented by daily vacation Bible school, summer camps, and special meetings for youth. Through the last decades of the twentieth century, the term "Christian education" was synonymous with these programs.

The Sunday school emerged at the time that a compartmentalized view of knowledge made its way into Europe and North America as an outgrowth of the Enlightenment. In this view, knowledge is divided into subject areas, such as literature, mathematics, the natural sciences, the social sciences, and religion. This approach gave birth to specialists. Education became the process of mastering specific subject areas.[6] A person went through a program to become a Christian in much the same way that ore goes through a program of mining, transportation, smelting, and forging to become a steel beam.

Preaching was also a major contributor to religious instruction for adults. However, the content of Sunday school lessons and the sermon were seldom related.

The Sunday school is based on a model of learning Christian discipleship by taking classes. Through the mid-twentieth century, classes were typically designed to impart information on a model of learning that is called "jug-mug." The teacher has a jug of knowledge from which the content of the lesson is poured into the mugs of students. The Sunday school lesson (in lecture format) typically included exposition of a Bible passage and interpretation of how to apply the meaning of the passage to today. Sunday school classes also provided pastoral care for the members, functioned as primary social circles, and gave members the opportunity for mission through class projects.

In the later part of the twentieth century, many Christian education programs followed changes in secular learning theory by shifting from the jug-mug pattern to more experiential approaches. Educators became increasingly aware that people learn in multiple modes that range from rational thought to intuition. Some people learn best in structured classroom settings following linear curricula while others learn best in environments in which they make their own discoveries. Some people learn by doing something and reflecting on it.

---

[6]This pattern of thought is related to the view of the world as a machine, which is typical of the Enlightenment. See Clark M. Williamson and Ronald J. Allen, *The Vital Church: Teaching, Worship, Community, Service* (St. Louis: Chalice Press, 1998), 78–80.

Many programs of Christian education implemented these insights by supplementing the lecture format with other modes of learning and curricula, such as discussion or learning by doing. For instance, Bible lectures were sometimes replaced by discussion of contemporary social issues. Programs of Christian education on the class model began to be offered at times other than Sunday morning. Small groups appeared for purposes ranging from Bible study to helping particular segments in the congregation learn about subject matters of interest (e.g., parenting skills). Short-term retreats and conferences increased in number.

However, despite such programming, the long-established denominations in North America are increasingly theologically illiterate. The mugs of the congregation have not been filled from the theological jugs of the Bible and Christian tradition.

## Christian Education through Congregational Practice

C. Ellis Nelson, a dynamic force in contemporary Christian education, sees three options for educational strategy in the contemporary church. The first is to revitalize the idea that education takes place through programs. This approach has the virtues of familiarity and clarity. This option, however, leaves Christian education segregated as only one segment of church life and does not recognize the formative power inherent in wider Christian community. The second option is to develop parochial schools. This option places students in an environment that is supposed to be self-consciously Christian. However, the long-established denominations do not have the money or motivation to establish such schools. Some people use parochial schools as a way to escape involvement in the wider society. The third option (endorsed in this chapter) is to view the whole life of the congregation as the agent of education.[7]

Many leading theorists think of Christian education as formation of the whole self—mind, heart, and behavior. Education was understood in much this way in the biblical period.[8] From this point of view, we can easily see how some of the practices function as moments of learning and teaching. For instance, Christian education

---

[7]C. Ellis Nelson, "Congregations' Educational Strategy," in *Carriers of Faith: Lessons from Congregational Studies,* ed. Carl S. Dudley, Jackson W. Carroll, and James P. Wind (Louisville: Westminster/John Knox Press, 1991), 163–69.

[8]Mary Elizabeth Mullino Moore captures this emphasis in her *Teaching from the Heart: Theology and Educational Method* (Minneapolis: Fortress Press, 1991), esp. 198–224; cf. Sara Little, *To Set One's Heart: Belief and Teaching in the Church* (Atlanta: John Knox Press, 1983).

obviously takes place when Christians tell the Christian story to one another by reading and hearing the Bible and the story of the church. These practices take place in Sunday school and Bible study groups and other settings that are formally designated as educational. Education also takes place in worship when the Bible is read, and during the sermon.

Christian education takes place whenever materials from the Bible and from the broader Christian tradition appear in the liturgy. Each time the Bible is used, it helps the congregation name the world from its perspective. For instance, when the congregation prays a common prayer of confession of sin, those who are praying learn how to offer such prayer. When the prayer of confession is followed by an assurance of forgiveness, the congregation learns that God forgives. The liturgy teaches in everything it does.

Another example comes from the practice of criticizing and resisting the principalities and powers that corrupt the divine intention for the relationship of humankind and nature. A group in a congregation is committed to Christian witness in the face of ecological abuse. When an industrial development threatens to disturb the local ecosystem, this group invites members of the congregation to protest. The sponsors provide members with information about why Christians should be concerned. In the process, many people in the congregation learn about ecological theology, the ecosystem, and the relationship between industrial development and the environment.

One of the freshest insights emerging from contemporary thinking about Christian education is that much Christian learning takes place in practices and settings that do not have education as their stated purpose and that do not resemble traditional educational events. Yet they are educational because they help members of the community discover ideas, feelings, and actions that are most important to the community and how to live those priorities. The preacher can help the congregation identify such moments and name the positive Christian learning that results.

For example, every morning before breakfast, my father read a passage from the Bible. Although he engaged in this practice for inspiration, he also learned the story in the Bible. He became able to place specific books and passages within the framework of the biblical narrative. Reading Bible passages raised questions about which he wanted to think and talk. Material from the daily readings helped him interpret his experience.

Carrying out acts of service and witness are a Christian practice. When one of our children was in elementary school, a dog attacked one of his classmates. The classmate had to have surgery. Soon, the classmate disappeared from school. Several months later, our son and I worked one evening at a shelter for homeless families. Our son was stunned to find the classmate and family in residence at the shelter. The classmate's family did not have health insurance. Medical bills created a household economic crisis that left them evicted from their apartment. The experience became a significant occasion of learning for our son. On the way home, he peppered me with questions about why his classmate's family had so little money and no insurance. In this encounter our son learned several things about the disparity between the biblical vision of justice and the economic system in North America.

Education can occur when Christians follow the practice of providing hospitality for one another and for strangers. Some friends housed a couple from Nicaragua when the couple was in Indianapolis for a meeting. Our friends became interested in Nicaragua and went there on several worktrips. When our congregation discussed a capital campaign to raise money to upgrade our local facilities, the members of this household spoke as a conscience to remind us that as we were spending money for spotlights in our sanctuary, people in Nicaragua needed housing, schools, and health care. The practice of hospitality became an experience of Christian education.

## *Christian Practice Forms the Congregation as Community*

Much Christian education earlier in this century was designed to help individual learners grow as individual Christians. Christian educators emphasize that Christian practices help form the church as *community*.[9] The practices create a reservoir of memory that is shared by the community as a whole. Bruce Birch, a professor of Bible, points out that shared memory forms identity and character by helping us realize who we are and, consequently, what we are to do.[10] The practices help pattern the feelings and actions of the community. The practices create shared experience through which we become aware of our bondedness with one another. Charles R. Foster, a leading Christian educator from Candler School of Theology thus entitled a

---

[9]Cf. Ronald J. Allen, Barbara Shires Blaisdell, and Scott Black Johnston, *Theology for Preaching: Authority, Truth, and Knowledge of God in a Postmodern Ethos* (Nashville: Abingdon Press, 1997), 137–60.

[10]Bruce C. Birch, "Memory in Congregational Life," in *Congregations: Their Power to Form and Transform,* ed. C. Ellis Nelson (Atlanta: John Knox Press, 1988), 29–30.

recent book *Educating Congregations*.[11] Thomas R. Hawkins speaks similarly of *The Learning Congregation*.[12]

Specific programs designed for Christian education should continue. Classes and other events for the purpose of Christian education will be a significant part of congregational life in the future. Programs of formal education often allow a group to consider the issue in a systematic way with depth and perspective that are necessary for full-bodied Christian interpretation. Programs appeal to people who are interested in specific subject matters. One of the greatest successes in today's church is gathering people into small groups on the basis of commonly shared traits or interests, such as young women, people with a shared physical condition, senior citizens, workers whose jobs take place at odd hours, and people who have suffered a particular abuse. These groups provide arenas within which Christian practices can take place. Further, they provide companionship and support, as well as opportunities for learning and mission. The agendas of such groups can often suggest agendas for sermons. Sermons can help raise the consciousness of the broader Christian community to such issues and can motivate people to want to learn about the issues studied in such groups. However, we can no longer view such efforts as the total educational ministry of the congregation.

## Preaching as Christian Education

Because everything that happens in a congregation teaches, the sermon teaches even when the preacher does not intend for it to do so. The sermon inevitably signals the congregation what the preacher believes is most important in the congregation's thinking, feeling, and doing. Consequently, preachers need to consider carefully the degree to which each sermon teaches the gospel. The sermon teaches formally and informally.

### *Formal Programs of Christian Education*

Formal programs of Christian education help create a reservoir of awareness within which the congregation receives and processes the sermon (and vice-versa). For instance, Sunday school may help members of the study group learn the content of Bible stories and an

---

[11]Charles R. Foster, *Educating Congregations: The Future of Christian Education* (Nashville: Abingdon Press, 1994).

[12]Thomas R. Hawkins, *The Learning Congregation: A New Vision of Leadership* (Louisville: Westminster John Knox Press, 1997).

interpretation of them. The class members may even associate emotional and relational dynamics of the group with the story.

However, in the last quarter of the twentieth century and the beginning of the twenty-first, preaching has seldom had a regular *direct* connection to formal programs of Christian education. People usually consider one subject matter in Sunday school or in some other program of Christian education, and then make their way to the sanctuary to participate in a sermon that focuses on another Bible passage or topic. The sermon and the lesson seldom have an opportunity to work in tandem.

A promising trend in recent preaching and the program model of Christian education is to coordinate the sermon with classroom activities so that the content of the sermon and the content of formal programs of Christian education relate to each other. This approach intensifies both the learning in the classroom and the congregation's participation in the sermon.

Such coordination requires planning. For instance, during the season when children and adults are preparing to be baptized or confirmed, the minister would easily preach from biblical texts and theological themes that relate to baptism, confirmation, or church membership. Such sermons likely would help interpret the importance of the steps at hand for the baptisands, confirmands, and other candidates for church membership. The sermons would also likely generate conversation in the congregation that would ripple beyond these groups. Other people in the congregation recollect and reaffirm their own baptisms or confirmations or decisions to participate in the body of Christ. They speak with the candidates, reinforcing the candidates' decisions, increasing their awareness of their shared history and mutual support with other believers, and deepening the candidates' experience.

Congregations that follow the Christian year and the Revised Common Lectionary can now find church school curricula in which the lessons in the Sunday school (or other learning settings) are based on the biblical passages that are appointed for each Sunday. The content and experience of Sunday school, the service of worship, and the sermon can be mutually enhancing.

However, this approach does not help participants gain know-ledge of the overarching biblical story, because texts from the lectionary do not tell the whole story in sequence. Students tend to get snippets of the Bible in isolation from one another. Furthermore, the theological rationale of the Christian year itself is seldom explained.

Non-lectionary-based curricula are available today that allow the sermon to coordinate with lessons in Sunday school. For instance, a Christian community that is using a church school curriculum that tells the story of the Bible over one or two years could use the same biblical texts and themes as the basis for preaching. A workshop rotation model of instruction could be used in which children, young people, and adults rotate through a series of activities—for example, drama, painting and sculpting, food preparation, computers, creative writing. That text for the Christian education hour could become the text for the sermon.

A congregation with a cadre of gifted teachers could create its own curriculum to coordinate with the sermon. For instance, a congregation could shape its own study materials, and sermons around the articles of the denomination's affirmation of faith. Each week might focus on a different article.

A new impulse in these matters is for the congregation to institute a midweek session in which the pastor, teachers, and worship planners engage the Bible passages, broader theological matters, and other materials for the upcoming Sunday.[13] I am familiar with a congregation that operates such a group with the requirements that (a) teachers must commit themselves to regular attendance, and (b) a participant must be teaching in the congregation. The group has become so energizing that the congregation has a perpetual waiting list of persons who want to teach so that they can become a part of the excitement of the group.

## Informal Christian Education

The preacher should help the congregation learn the expanded view of Christian education that is emerging in our time. Occasional sermons can help members of the congregation become aware of how learning takes place throughout the system and can alert members of the congregation to take advantage of such educational moments.

The sermon is the most consistently well-attended event in the church. The preacher can help the congregation remember (or learn) the content of the gospel, its norms, and the character and mission of the community. The preacher needs to bring these basic gospel

---

[13]C. Ellis Nelson develops such an approach in detail under the designation of "Central Study Group" in his *How Faith Matures* (Louisville: Westminster/John Knox Press, 1989), 204–30.

perspectives into sermons fairly often because congregations so easily lose sight of them and because new people are continuously coming into the congregation and need to learn the congregation's foundational theological worldview. The sermon can then help the community consider the degree to which its life is consistent with that vision. At what points is the congregation's system teaching the gospel? How can such qualities be reinforced? At what points is the congregational system teaching values and practices that are contrary to the gospel? What does the congregation need to do to correct aspects of its system that work against the gospel?

### Explicit, Hidden, and Null Curricula

Contemporary Christian educators provide the preacher with a useful way of thinking about what the congregational system teaches when they speak of explicit curriculum, hidden curriculum, and null curriculum.[14] The explicit curriculum includes actual curriculum materials that are used in Bible school classes, small groups, and other formal occasions. Systems thinking urges us to realize that the explicit curriculum consists more broadly of what the church aims to teach throughout its system. The preacher needs to help the congregation assess its explicit curriculum from the perspective of appropriateness to the gospel, intelligibility, and moral plausibility.

Hidden curriculum includes what I elsewhere call informal and tacit qualities. The hidden curriculum is what is taught in addition to (or sometimes in place of) the explicit curriculum. From the hidden curriculum the congregation learns what is *actually* expected of them. For instance, a formal curriculum may encourage members to do business with Christian establishments. The hidden dimension may be that church members are expected to patronize businesses owned by other members. A preacher must help the congregation recognize the hidden curricula at work in the congregational system.

A null curriculum, as its name implies, is material that is *not* taught when it could or should be. By not explicitly dealing with a theme, a congregation teaches that the theme is not important. The results are often contrary to the gospel. For instance, a church may not teach that, in Christ, relationships between women and men are egalitarian. Consequently, patriarchy persists. The reasons for null curriculum may be plotted on a spectrum. At one end, null curriculum may result from something as innocent as the fact that the community does not know that certain materials should be taught. At the other end of the

---

[14]On these designations, see Elliot Eisner, *The Educational Imagination: On the Design and Evaluation of School Programs,* 2d ed. (New York: Macmillan, 1985), 88–108.

spectrum, null curriculum may result from pernicious complicity by leaders to prevent the community from knowing key materials. The leaders maintain power by trying to keep the congregation in ignorance. The preacher's vocation includes helping the congregation identify the null curricula in its life. What are the reasons for this null curricula? What steps can the congregation take to rectify these omissions?

## *The Sermon Interprets Christian Practices*

The preacher is called to interpret Christian practices in the sermon so that the congregation can become cognizant of ways that the practices serve the various curricula of the church and nourish the life system of the congregation with the gospel. These practices directly form Christian content. They help the congregation think, feel, and act as Christians. They also model how the congregation can interact in a Christian way with texts, doctrines, situations, or practices. The practice of the practices in the sermon helps sensitize the congregation to ways that they can put the practices into practice in other settings in the church and world. For instance, the pattern of analyzing a social situation in the sermon becomes a pattern by which the community can analyze other situations.

As a member of the community set aside for this purpose through ordination, the preacher tells the Christian story to others. The preacher helps the congregation hear this story through the Bible and through the history of the church with an eye and ear toward interpreting how the Bible and Christian history and theology are significant for the church and world today. These tasks have two important dimensions:

1. The sermon can perform a basic *informational function* by helping the congregation learn or recall the stories of the Bible and the church. Many Christians today do not possess basic information about the Bible and Christian belief and life. Many congregations today are biblically and theologically illiterate.

2. The sermon can help the congregation interpret the *significance* of the Bible and Christian history and theology for the contemporary church and world. The preacher leads the congregation in a conversation that identifies the claims of the gospel, and the implications of those claims.[15] How

---

[15]For a conversational paradigm of preaching, see my *Interpreting the Gospel: An Introduction to Preaching* (St. Louis: Chalice Press, 1998), 63–95.

does the Christian story help the congregation make sense of its experience in the world? How does the experience of the congregation help it make sense of the Christian story?

## *Attentive Listening Plays a Significant Role*

The preparation of the sermon should include the pastor's practice of attentive listening to the congregation and the world.[16] The pastor listens to what others say. What are their stated questions? the values and behaviors to which they are formally committed? their hopes? fears? A pastor can often gain access to this information by general pastoral listening in the course of pastoral calling, visiting people on their jobs, paying attention to the comments that people make. Conscientious pastors can also interview members of the congregation on these matters in personal or small group interviews, as well as through the use of survey instruments.

Attentive listening may lead the preacher to recognize questions, needs, and issues that should be addressed from the pulpit. A preacher can formulate a series of sermons in response to concerns of the congregation.

Attentive listening has several learning and teaching functions. When the sermon manifests attentive listening, it teaches the congregation how to listen to others. Attentive listening helps the pastor correlate the gospel with the situation of the congregation. Attentive listening includes the listener's reflecting to other persons what the listener is hearing. In its most overt form, the listener says to the other, "I hear you saying...." In its less overt forms, the listener may include material in the discourse that signals the others in the dialogue that they have been heard. This custom allows listeners to confirm that they correctly understand the others by giving others the opportunity to confirm or correct the listener's impressions. It allows others in the conversation to realize that they have been heard and understood. In the depersonalized culture of North America, this recognition can be a significant moment of learning. "I am not alone in this world. Someone understands me. I understand others. We are bound together in community."

A minister is called to take a leading role in helping the community struggle together to make sense of the many interlocking

---

[16]For careful approaches to listening to the congregation, see John McClure, *The Round-Table Pulpit: Where Preaching and Leadership Meet* (Nashville: Abingdon Press, 1995); Stephen Farris, *Preaching that Matters: The Bible and Our Lives* (Louisville: Westminster John Knox Press, 1998), 25–38; Nora Tubbs Tisdale, *Preaching as Local Theology and Folk Art,* Fortress Resources in Preaching (Minneapolis: Fortress Press, 1997).

contexts in which the congregation lives. The sermon can help the congregation identify these contexts and their relationships with one another and with the gospel. These contexts include household, neighborhood, congregation, city, state, nation, globe, and universe.

Through the homily, the preacher can help the congregation recognize and criticize the principalities and powers that corrupt the divine intention for the world. Many people today think that God intends the brokenness of the world. They do not recognize that the world has deviated from God's desire for the world to be a place of abundance, mutuality, community, and support for all. The sermon can help the congregation learn God's intention. Sermons can help the community name and understand the forces that foul the divine intention. Preaching can lead the community to identify ways in which we can be in partnership with God to pursue the divine intentions.

The sermon is part of a teaching and learning environment when it helps the congregation learn how to practice the practices. For example, preaching can help members of the community learn why it is important to pray, how to do so, and on what they can depend as a result of prayer. The message can teach the community why confession of sin is important, how to confess to God and one another, and how to seek forgiveness and reconciliation. A homily can lead the community to understand the significance of tolerating one another in failure and in encouraging one another to embody more fully the life to which God calls, and it can reveal why, from the perspective of the gospel, we sometimes suffer with and for one another and for our neighbors. Preaching can help the congregation name acts of service and witness that the church can carry out, and can help empower the community to do so.

## Implications for Preachers

In recent years, the church has begun to rediscover that Christian education is not so much a program within the congregation as a phenomenon that takes place throughout the congregational system, especially through Christian practices. The preacher has several distinct opportunities and responsibilities to enhance the role of the sermon as educational moment and to work with other elements of the congregation to enhance the educational qualities of the congregational system. The preacher can

- help the congregation acquire fundamental information about Christian tradition (e.g., the content of the Bible, Christian history, Christian doctrine, and theological method for Christian living and witness today).

- help the congregation discover both how to understand life today from the perspective of Christian tradition, and how to reinterpret that tradition from the viewpoint of the contemporary world (i.e., how to interpret the Bible for the sake of the church and world today).

- help the congregation bring to consciousness the education that takes place throughout the congregational system, in particular in the Christian practices.

- provide basic information about Christian practices and their educational role in Christian life. What are the practices? Why are they important in shaping us? How do we put them into practice? How do we sustain their continued practice?

- ask of every event and relationship, What are we teaching here? Does it reinforce Christian identity and witness?

- take account of ways that educational events in aspects of the congregation's life outside of worship and preaching can (and should) affect the content of sermons. What do other events suggest that the congregation needs to learn via the sermon?

- work with other congregational leaders to find ways whereby the sermon can coordinate with other programs.

- uphold those who are taking formal teaching duties in the church and help the congregation to involve more people in those roles.

- initiate groups of other clergy or people in the congregation with whom to study the Bible lesson (or other material) that is the foundation of the upcoming sermons.

- review what theological and ethical curricula the sermons are teaching explicitly, implicitly, and in their null mode.

- cultivate attentive listening for him- or herself and help the congregation become better able to engage in this practice.

## Implications for the Theory of Christian Education

Christian educators can help pastors realize that all sermons teach. All sermons help the congregation name the world. Christian educators can encourage preachers to ask whether sermons are helping the congregation name the world in terms of the gospel.

Educators can develop materials that help preachers recognize qualities from contemporary educational theory that can help sermons become optimal events of learning and teaching.[17] For example, how can a preacher effectively use questions to help the congregation engage a subject matter? A description of positive qualities that the sermon can manifest for teaching and learning should be accompanied by an analysis of things that preachers sometimes do that frustrate learning.

Christian educators in conjunction with systematic theologians and congregational members can help preachers develop a theological curriculum that can be taught from the pulpit. What are the key ideas about God, Christ, the Holy Spirit, the church, and the world that a congregation needs to know to be able to be an optimal Christian community? How can contemporary educational theory help us plan sermons to give the congregation the best opportunities to interact with those doctrines?

Christian educators could help preachers find a way of assessing the impact (or lack thereof) of sermons in congregations. Preachers currently have few methods of evaluating the degree to which communication and learning take place through preaching. Educators, especially in secular settings, have developed methods for evaluating the relative success of educational events and could help preachers ponder similar evaluating mechanisms for gauging the degree to which sermons are taking root in the hearts, minds, and wills of the congregations, and suggesting remedial things that pastors can do to increase the likelihood that sermons will be effective events of learning and teaching.

## Suggestions for Further Reading

Allen, Ronald J. *The Teaching Sermon*. Nashville: Abingdon Press, 1995. Basic introduction to the sermon as an event of learning and teaching.

Dykstra, Craig. *Growing in Faith: Education and Christian Practices* (Louisville: Westminster John Knox Press, 1999). Comprehensive introduction to Christian practices as educational.

Foster, Charles R. *Educating Congregations: The Future of Christian Education* (Nashville: Abingdon Press, 1994). Emphasizes congregation as a community of teaching and learning.

---

[17]I have taken some basic steps in this direction in *The Teaching Sermon* (Nashville: Abingdon Press, 1995), 39–62, but preachers need much more help.

Moore, Mary Elizabeth Mullino. *Teaching from the Heart: Theology and Educational Method* (Minneapolis: Fortress Press, 1991). Explores relationship between theology and educational approaches; cf. her *Education for Continuity and Change* (Nashville: Abingdon Press, 1983).

Osmer, Richard R. *A Teachable Spirit: Recovering the Teaching Office in the Church* (Louisville: Westminster/John Knox Press, 1990). Historical overview of the teaching in Christian community with contemporary implications.

# 3

# THE PREACHER AS PASTOR

A generation ago many pastors thought of pastoral care and pastoral counseling as synonymous. The minister engaged in pastoral care by employing psychotherapy in one-on-one counseling sessions, in hospital calling, or in ministry with persons in crisis.

However, a primary cutting edge in thinking about pastoral care is the rediscovery that the congregation itself should be the primary agent of pastoral care. Indeed, through most of the church's history, pastoral care has referred to all that the church does to build up the community in the gospel, such as preaching, teaching, pastoral calling. In a more focused way, pastoral care has sometimes referred to the work of the community in helping persons in difficult circumstances. The church has often taken care to mean comfort, but the Christian community sometimes expresses care through helping members correct thoughts, feelings, and behaviors. A movement is underway to help the church recover these emphases while integrating pastoral counseling into them.

This chapter explores ways in which preaching can join the recent recovery of the notion that the life of the congregation can function as a system of pastoral care. I first recall the historic notion of pastoral care. After a critique of the drift away from the historic notion into the restricted equation of pastoral care and pastoral counseling, the chapter considers preventive and healing dimensions in pastoral care.

I note ways that the renewed vision of pastoral care can contribute to preaching, and ways in which preaching can contribute to pastoral care. Christian practices are important throughout.

## Shepherding in the Bible and Christian Tradition

Our terms *pastoral* and *pastor* derive from a root that means "shepherd." The work of a shepherd is a pattern for pastoral work in the congregation. This background reveals the broad, systemic understanding of pastoral care as all that church does to help the congregation recognize and respond to the gospel.

Psalm 23 pictures the vocation of the shepherd.[1] The psalm assumes that the sheep and the shepherd are well acquainted, and that the sheep trust the shepherd. The shepherd finds sources of nutrition for the flock (green pastures, still waters) and guides them along safe routes (right paths). The shepherd is a guide in difficulty (the dark valley). The shepherd carries a rod to protect the community, and a staff to discipline the sheep. The table is a pasture from which the shepherd has removed noxious weeds. When a briar wounds the head of a sheep, the shepherd anoints it with oil, that is, with a medicine, and gives it a medicinal drink (the overflowing cup). The shepherd sometimes expresses care in quiet, soothing ways. At other times, a shepherd expresses care through discipline. The shepherd must sometimes use the staff to say no. The shepherd cares for the sheep by finding and creating conditions under which the flock can produce.

This full-bodied understanding of pastoral care is evident when biblical writers employ shepherding imagery to speak of care in the community. Ezekiel 34 contrasts true shepherds and false.[2] The true shepherds of Israel exercise the full range of shepherding. They help the community realize both God's promise to be faithful and God's call to live justly. Shepherds call the people to account when the people violate the covenant by practicing idolatry or injustice. They call the community to repent.

By contrast, the false shepherds allow the sheep to scatter and to become weak and sick. They allow the sheep to become food for wild animals. They allow the lost sheep to remain lost. They reinterpret the covenant to serve their immediate ends. They overlook idolatry and injustice. They do not call the people to repent. False shepherds

---

[1]Ronald J. Allen, "The Relationship between the Pastoral and the Prophetic in Preaching," *Encounter* 49 (1988): 176–78; id., *The Teaching Sermon* (Nashville: Abingdon Press, 1995), 120–25. We should note that shepherds in the world of the Bible were sometimes regarded negatively.

[2]Cf. Jeremiah 23:1–4 and Zechariah 11:4–17.

even eat the sheep. Because of a shortage of true shepherds, God personally assumes responsibility for the flock of Ezekiel's day.

In the parable of the good shepherd (Matthew 18:10–14), Matthew explicitly identifies the leaders of the Matthean community as shepherds (vv. 10–14). Such leaders are to call the community to discipleship (vv. 1–5). They are to teach the community to avoid sin (vv. 6–10). The members of the community are to seek those who wander by confronting the sin of violating relationships in community. Christians are to forgive and reconcile (vv. 15–22; cf. Matthew 5:21–26). Christians who do not reconcile are to be treated as Gentiles. These actions demonstrate care, for they warn the flock that members will be eternally condemned for failing to reconcile with one another (vv. 23–35).

The gospel of John uses a similar image to describe the relationship of Jesus with the community (10:1–42). The essence of care is to give one's life (vv. 14–15). This motif is behind Jesus' call to Peter, "Feed my lambs" (John 21:15–19). Peter is to be a shepherd after the model of Jesus. In the Fourth Gospel, pastoral care is self-giving love.

In the book of Acts, Paul compares elders to shepherds. They express their shepherding care by teaching the whole purpose of God. The shepherds are to contend with the savage wolves (false teachers) that come into the community from the outside. They are to expose distortions of the truth that arise within the congregation (Acts 20:18–35).

In the Bible, then, to be pastoral is to engage in the full range of activities that are necessary to build up the community in the gospel so that the community can enjoy the fruit of the gospel in its own life, and so that the community can witness to the gospel in the larger world.[3]

This general picture of pastoral care continues until the early twentieth century. A major historian of the pastoral vocation captures its essence in a chapter titled "Discipline and Consolation."[4]

Gregory the Great (540–604 C.E.) gives this approach to the pastoral work an eloquent and sustained exposition in *Pastoral Care.*[5]

---

[3]For assessment of shepherding as a way to image pastoral care, see G. Lee Ramsey, Jr., *Care-full Preaching: From Sermon to Caring Community* (St. Louis: Chalice Press, 2000), 31–49; cf. Carroll Watkins Ali, "A Womanist Search for Sources," in *Feminist and Womanist Pastoral Theology,* ed. Bonnie Miller-McLemore and Brita Gill-Austern (Nashville: Abingdon Press, 1999), 51–64.

[4]John T. McNeill, *A History of the Cure of Souls* (New York: Harper and Brothers, 1951), 88.

[5]Gregory the Great, *Pastoral Care,* trans. Henry Davis, Ancient Christian Writers Series, vol. 11 (Westminster, Md.: Newman Press, 1950).

This book was a benchmark for pastoral work for almost a thousand years. Gregory specifically focuses on *preaching* as a basic expression of pastoral care. Gregory's axiom is that the care of the pastor for the congregation, and the care of the members of the congregation for one another, are to reflect God's care for the church through Jesus Christ. As Christ became a servant, so Christians are to serve one another.[6]

Each pastoral case is to be handled differently, for each has its own dynamics. "Often, for instance, what is profitable to some harms others. Thus, too, herbs which nourish some animals kill others; gentle hissing that calms horses excites young puppies; medicine that alleviates one disease, aggravates another…"[7] The preacher needs to deal both with the feelings of the parishioner, and with the parishioner's behavior and social circumstances.[8]

Gregory notes that a quality that appears to be a virtue in a person may conceal a limitation. For instance, a person who is tolerant of others may have an inadequate understanding of Christian faith and its requirements. Thus, the pastoral community sometimes needs to help a person or group name these undertows and take actions that bring them into conformity with Christian vision.[9]

This comprehensive understanding of care continues in the Reformation. For both Luther and Calvin, the goal of pastoral care is to help the congregation learn to trust God and to live accordingly.[10] Preaching and the sacraments are key to assuring people that they are in God's grace and to helping them respond with lives that reflect that grace. The sermon is to instruct the congregation in the ways of God. The knowledge of God that comes through these means is essential for helping the community live faithfully, and for helping members make their way through the difficulties of sickness and chaotic relationships. Both Luther and Calvin call for Christians to console and confront one another as necessary. From this perspective, Calvin's third use of the law (namely, that the law instructs people in how to live in ways that are faithful to God and that promote godly community) promotes pastoral care. The elders in Geneva observed their companion citizens every day, not as spies but with an eye toward those who needed particular forms of care. Calvin stressed repentance

---

[6]Thomas C. Oden, *Care of Souls in the Classic Tradition,* Theology and Pastoral Care Series (Philadelphia: Fortress Press, 1984), 56–57.

[7]Gregory the Great, *Pastoral Care,* 89.

[8]Ibid., 68.

[9]Ibid., 55–56.

[10]On Luther and Calvin, see McNeill, *A History of the Cure of Souls,* 163–76, 197–209.

as a means toward reconciliation not only with God but also with others in the community. Both Luther and Calvin talked with individuals and engaged in extensive correspondence as means of pastoral care.

Liston O. Mills, who taught pastoral counseling at the Divinity School of Vanderbilt University before retirement, identifies several distinct currents in the post-Reformation churches.[11] The Roman Catholic tradition continued to emphasize participation in the sacraments as the church's primary means of providing pastoral care. Through penance and reconciliation, pastoral care often took on a social dimension.[12]

Lutherans were to express pastoral care for one another by teaching, exhorting, rebuking, and consoling. The community was guided in these activities through preaching and public worship. The Lutheran pietists added small-group experiences as arenas within which to encourage one another on the journey from despair to hope.[13]

Anglicans, epitomized by George Herbert in *The Country Parson*, regarded the typical week as representing the essence of pastoral care.[14] On Sunday, the congregation gathered for preaching in the morning. The afternoon was for teaching, reconciling quarrels, and visiting the sick. On weekdays, members called on one another for upbuilding (examining, counseling, admonishing).[15] Anglicanism gave birth to the Wesleyan small groups (classes) that mediated pastoral care in the classical sense by offering education in the Bible and doctrine, as well as inspiration, edification, accountability, and prayer.

Richard Baxter is the most important figure in pastoral care in the Reformed churches. The Reformed pastor, according to Baxter, offered pastoral care through preaching, the sacraments, and intensive visitation in homes and workplaces instructing persons in the ways of God.[16]

---

[11]Liston O. Mills, "Pastoral Care (History, Traditions, and Definitions)," in *Dictionary of Pastoral Care and Counseling,* ed. Rodney J. Hunter (Nashville: Abingdon Press, 1990), 839–41. Mills adapts these categories from E. Brooks Holifield, *A History of Pastoral Care in America: From Salvation to Self-Realization* (Nashville: Abingdon Press, 1983). Mills adds the congregational category to Holifield's taxonomy.

[12]Mills, "Pastoral Care," 839–40; on Roman Catholicism, cf. McNeill, *A History of the Cure of Souls,* 287–306.

[13]Mills, "Pastoral Care," 840; on Lutheranism, cf. McNeill, *A History of the Cure of Souls,* 177–91.

[14]George Herbert, *A Priest to the Temple, or The Country Parson* (New York: Paulist Press, 1981, o.p. 1652).

[15]Mills, "Pastoral Care," 840–41; on Anglicanism, cf. McNeill, *A History of the Cure of Souls,* 218–46.

[16]Richard Baxter, *The Reformed Pastor* (London: SCM Press, 1956; o.p. 1656).

The Congregational churches emphasized the congregation as a community of care, or mutual edification. Congregational communities "were held together by covenants" in which each person agreed to watch over the others, to edify one another, to bear one another's burdens, and to express concern for the sick, the widow, the orphan, and others in various forms of difficulty. Pastoral care was intended to provoke changes of thought and behavior to help people live more fully in the gospel. The Congregational churches also disciplined members.[17]

Friedrich Schliermacher (1768–1834) highlighted an important dimension in this discussion. Schliermacher conceived of theological inquiry as similar to a tree, having three phases: philosophical theology (roots), biblical and historical studies (trunk), practical theology (branches). For Schliermacher, practical theology meant embodying the Christian life made possible by philosophical and biblical-historical insights. The roots and trunk of Christian tradition are to yield the fruit of Christian life. Consequently, pastoral care should be a critical discipline that helps the community form, implement, and continuously advocate a Christian vision of life. A contemporary movement in practical theology recaptures elements of this vision.[18]

Pastoral care is expressed through worship, relationships, the shaping of the congregation, and decisions of leadership, and even through mission.[19] Christian tradition views pastoral care as a function of the congregational life system.

## From Community Formation to Individual Therapy

A change, symbolized by the work of Sigmund Freud, took place in the late nineteenth and early twentieth centuries. Freud focused on the individual as psychological being as locus for determining meaning in life.[20] The movement toward individualism had been underway since the Enlightenment. As a part of this cultural trend in the late nineteenth and early twentieth centuries, some congregations came to think of Christian faith as a private affair. A congregation was a collection of individuals. Prior to this time, congregations had

---

[17]Mills, "Pastoral Care," 842. On Congregationalists, cf. McNeill, *A History of the Cure of Souls,* 270–80.

[18]For literature, see Gijsbert E. J. Dingemans, "Practical Theology in the Academy: A Contemporary Overview," *Journal of Religion* 76 (1996): 82–96.

[19]Holifield, *A History of Pastoral Care,* passim.

[20]Cf. Allen, in Allen, Blaisdell, and Johnston, *Theology for Preaching: Authority, Truth, and Knowledge of God in a Postmodern Ethos* (Nashville: Abingdon Press, 1997), 137–40; and Allison Stokes, *Ministry After Freud* (New York: Pilgrim Press, 1985).

tended to think of themselves as communities. A Christian was a person-in-community.

As a part of the emergence of the psychological milieu in North America, pastoral care came to be identified, narrowly, with pastoral counseling. Many seminaries contain a department of pastoral care that focuses on counseling in which the pastor enters into one-on-one relationships. Such endeavors sometimes take their aims less from Christian norms and more from the notions of the self that emerged from the discipline of psychology.

E. Brooks Holifield, noted church historian, traces a shift from the understanding of pastoral care as leading to salvation to a goal that he summarizes as "self-realization," that is, discovering and giving complete expression to the true self.[21] The counselor attempts to help the counselee identify the heart of this self and to achieve liberation from forces that restrict the self from being all that it can be (e.g., personal inhibitions, social mores, religious strictures). In some circles, personal subjective feelings were the only norms by which to gauge the degree to which one was reaching self-realization. Philip Rieff gave this movement a memorable moniker, "the triumph of the therapeutic." It could as easily be called the triumph of individualism.[22]

Psychologist Carl Rogers emphasized acceptance as an important part of the environment that makes self-realization possible.[23] Rogers asserted that the counselor should have unconditional positive regard for the counselee. The counselor should never voice objections to the counselee's thoughts, feelings, or behaviors, lest these objections create an authoritarian repression of the counselee's growth.

In a common theological rationale for this approach, the true self was said to be an aspect of the image of God. Therapy restores this image and frees the self to express it fully. This restoration can only take place in an atmosphere of unconditional acceptance. Through Jesus Christ, God has given us a sign of the divine unconditional positive regard.[24] The relationship of counselor to

---

[21]Holifield, *A History of Pastoral Care,* 288–94.

[22]Philip Rieff, *The Triumph of the Therapeutic: Uses of Faith after Freud* (Chicago: University of Chicago Press, 1987, o.p. 1966).

[23]Holifield, *A History of Pastoral Care,* 294–306.

[24]For the extent to which the psychological perspectives influenced pastoral counseling, see ibid., 300-306; cf. Rodney Hunter, "The Therapeutic Tradition of Pastoral Care and Counseling," in *Pastoral Care and Social Conflict: Essays in Honor of Charles V. Gerkin,* ed. Pamela D. Couture and Rodney J. Hunter (Nashville: Abingdon Press, 1995), 17–31.

counselee can mediate this unconditional acceptance of God to the counselee.

Some ministers even began to think of preaching as "counseling on a group scale,"[25] with the sermon modeled on the counseling session. The preacher helped the congregation deal with real needs faced by individuals. The preacher spoke as an individual to individuals. Preachers sometimes offered little more than psychological theory, or their own opinions, as help with the presenting problem.[26]

The therapeutic model of counseling frequently operates in theological amnesia. It reinforces the individualistic understanding of the self. It understands the goal of life to be feeling good about oneself without reference to others who transcend the self (e.g., God, the neighbor). It seldom takes account of social context.

## The Congregation as Community of Care

The emergence of the psychological disciplines opened an important dialogue between religion and psychology that should continue. Yet, by the 1970s, pastoral theologians became uneasy about aspects of this movement.[27] A bold new initiative in contemporary pastoral theology is to envision the church as a community of care.[28] Furthermore, today's leaders in pastoral care seek to recover the notion

---

[25]Edmund Holt Linn, *Preaching as Counseling: The Unique Method of Harry Emerson Fosdick* (Valley Forge, Pa.: Judson Press, 1966).

[26]For critique, see Donald Capps, *Pastoral Counseling and Preaching: A Quest for an Integrated Ministry* (Philadelphia: The Westminster Press, 1980), 17–18, and Ramsey, *Care-full Preaching*, 12–23.

[27]Representative of critiques are Don S. Browning, *The Moral Context of Pastoral Care* (Philadelphia: The Westminster Press, 1976); Charles V. Gerkin, *Widening the Horizons: Pastoral Responses to a Fragmented Society* (Philadelphia: The Westminster Press, 1986); id., *Prophetic Pastoral Practice: A Christian View of Life Together* (Nashville: Abingdon Press, 1991); id., *Introduction to Pastoral Care* (Nashville: Abingdon Press, 1997); John Patton, *Pastoral Care in Context: An Introduction to Pastoral Care* (Louisville: Westminster/John Knox Press, 1993); Roy Herndon SteinhoffSmith, *The Mutuality of Care* (St. Louis: Chalice Press, 1999); James Dittes, *Pastoral Counseling: A Brief Introduction* (Louisville: Westminster John Knox Press, 1999). For efforts to recover this sense in preaching, see Gary D. Stratman, *Pastoral Preaching: Timeless Truth For Changing Needs* (Nashville: Abingdon Press, 1983); Ronald Allen, "The Relationship Between the Pastoral and the Prophetic in Preaching"; Ramsey, *Care-full Preaching;* David G. Buttrick, *A Captive Voice: The Liberation of Preaching* (Louisville: Westminster/John Knox Press, 1994), 13–14, 46–47, 72, 103–5.

[28]As representative of the turn toward the community as agent of care, see Kathleen D. Billman, "Pastoral Care as an Art of Community," in *The Arts of Ministry: Feminist-Womanist Approaches,* ed. Christie Cozad Neuger (Louisville: Westminster John Knox Press, 1996), 10–38; Patton, *Pastoral Care in Context;* Gerkin, *Prophetic Pastoral Practice* and *Introduction to Pastoral Care.*

that all that happens in the community can express pastoral care, especially Christian practices. Some care is formal, while some is informal and even tacit. Pastoral counseling is one expression of pastoral care. I distinguish two modes of care: preventive and healing.

## *Preventive Pastoral Care*

Most pastoral care is preventive and takes place as the congregational system helps the community become a healthy theological body. In order to be a healthy body, the church needs a vivid sense of the presence of God and a clear understanding of the nature and extent of the help that God provides in every life situation. Such preparation both helps persons function in everyday situations and prepares them to face life disturbances.

The Christian practice of weekly worship is pastoral care, for instance, because it represents the relationship of God to the world.[29] Just as God is with us as assuring presence in bread and cup in the sanctuary, so God is with us as assuring presence in every life situation. Interpreting the Bible and telling the Christian story to one another give preventive pastoral care by building up faith that can guide us when life is smooth and that can help us interpret disruptive circumstances.

Several Christian practices take on the quality of pastoral care when they help people in the congregation bond as community. People can turn to one another, intensify their celebrations, encourage one another in witness, and support one another when life tumbles in. The Christian practices of tolerating one another, suffering with (and for) one another, providing hospitality, and listening to one another are frequently key to a church's becoming such a community. The formal educational program of the church sometimes results in groups' (e.g., Bible school classes) becoming such communities.

To people anchored in community, the savage storms of life are no less painful than to persons who are not anchored in such communities. But anchored people have a firm mooring on which to hold.

Congregational leaders need to assess regularly the degree to which the life system of the congregation forms vital Christians. Congregations need to determine whether they are helping Christians formulate a vision of divine love and justice that is adequate for ordinary circumstances and for guiding them in crisis.

---

[29]Cf. William H. Willimon, *Worship as Pastoral Care* (Nashville: Abingdon Press, 1979), and Elaine Ramshaw, *Ritual and Pastoral Care,* Theology and Pastoral Care Series (Philadelphia: Fortress Press, 1987).

My pastoral experience illustrates the importance of this task. I repeatedly heard questions like these in the face of difficulty: "Why did this tragedy happen?" "Why did God do this horrible thing to me?" "Why is God angry with me?" "Why has God abandoned me?" "Why…why…why?" Such a situation is seldom an occasion when a person or group is ready to engage in the hard theological thinking required to respond to such bone-deep aches. Emotions are so tender that presence and assurance are the most pastoral care that a person can receive. However, such questions indicate that the church has not engaged in sufficient preventive theological pastoral care. People should have the resources in place to deal with such questions when disruption occurs.

A preacher could help the congregation in this regard by regularly dealing with foundational questions. For instance, years ago Robert McAfee Brown organized a book around questions such as, How does God make Godself known? What makes Jesus so important? What is the cross all about? Why is there evil? How can I be changed? What does the Bible have to say about sex and marriage? What does the Christian do about war?[30] In response to such questions, a preacher could easily develop series of sermons that function as preventive pastoral care covering a wide range of issues.

## *Healing Pastoral Care*

Some pastoral care in the congregation is healing. A person who is sick goes to a physician. The physician diagnoses the problem and prescribes medicines. The medical staff may help the patient recover completely, regain partial health and learn to live successfully with diminished powers, or contemplate the end of life.

Healing pastoral care is called forth by circumstances that make it difficult for a person or group to name and benefit from the divine promise of love and call for justice. This form of pastoral care seeks to help people regain the capacity to recognize and receive God's love, and to live in right relationship with God, themselves, and others.

Toward this end, Kathy Black, a professor at Claremont School of Theology, distinguishes between cure and healing. Pastoral care cannot always result in cure, that is, complete restoration of the self. A husband who has abandoned a family may not come home. When a leg has been removed, it can seldom be reattached. But pastoral care can move toward healing, that is, helping people come to terms

---

[30]Robert McAfee Brown, *The Bible Speaks to You* (Philadelphia: The Westminster Press, 1955), 5–6.

with their situations so as to perceive God's supportive presence and to live fully.[31] In some circumstances pastoral care can help people experience the peace that passes understanding. In other situations, the most that pastoral care can do is to assure persons that God shares their suffering and is faithfully present. In still other situations, a word violates the silence that surrounds someone in anguish. A pastoral caregiver can only stand in silence with that person.

Several factors lead contemporary pastoral theologians to think of healing pastoral care as the work of the whole community, not just the private province of the pastor. According to the priesthood of all believers, the church is supposed to be a community of mutual care. The number of needs in a congregation can easily expand beyond the capacity of the pastoral staff to respond to them all. Many needs in a congregation do not require professional attention. I once heard a pastoral psychotherapist say that many people do not need a therapist as much as they need a friend in the gospel.

The church often provides healing pastoral care through formal means. Some congregations offer pastoral counseling by appointment with the pastor or though a pastoral counseling center. Christian practices constitute many aspects of formal acts of healing pastoral care. A funeral service, for instance, can have this quality. A sermon can offer a meaningful interpretation of the significance of the death. Some church functions mediate healing care by providing hospitality. At the time of death, for instance, many congregations serve a meal. While the food itself is welcome, the meal is a symbol that the church is a community of care. Many congregations train lay leaders to represent the gospel with persons in the hospital and other crises.

Much healing pastoral care can take place in informal and tacit ways as people relate to one another in everyday settings. Christian practices can often be powerful agents of healing pastoral care. For instance, I have a friend who was once vexed by a relationship. My friend was jogging with someone from church when this problem came into their conversation. The other runner listened attentively, asking a few perceptive questions. By the end of the run, my friend knew what to do: confess sin in the relationship and seek reconciliation.

I have another friend who is a pastor in a congregation in which a person lost a job when a corporate staff was downsized. The

---

[31]Kathy Black, *A Healing Homiletic: Preaching and Disability* (Nashville: Abingdon Press, 1996), 50–54. Paul Scott Wilson contends that Black too quickly abandons the notion of cure as a possibility in *Homiletic* 23/2 (1997): 19–20.

unemployed person suffered a loss of self-esteem. This person went to a job placement seminar sponsored by the church. At that time, the congregation invited the unemployed person to serve as the chair of a mission event. Months later the person reported that receiving the invitation to chair the mission event was a crucial act of pastoral care. "It certified that someone had faith in me."

### Pastoral Calling

A renewed emphasis on pastoral calling is needed today. Although ministers and other congregational leaders usually call on parishioners in the hospital and at other times of trauma, few pastors today routinely visit the homes and work sites of the congregation. Such encounters can be a means of detailing the personal and social situations of members of the community and can provide insight into issues that are important to the congregation. These visits also strengthen the bond between the caller and the called on.

Pastors may need to plan carefully for pastoral calling, especially in urban settings.[32] Many people are out of the home much of the time. In households in which spouses, partners, children, and other inhabitants often have multiple careers, the whole household may seldom be home at the same time. Many urban apartment buildings and businesses have elaborate security systems. While ministers can engage in a certain amount of pastoral relationship with technologically capable people through e-mail and other media, many people find a face-to-face encounter to be irreplaceable. The minister seeking to engage in pastoral calling needs to arrange for such visits ahead of time.

The vision of the church as caring community suggests that members of the congregation need to call on one another. The preacher needs both to encourage people to call on one another and to interpret this activity so that people understand that it is more than socializing.

### Pastoral Counseling Helps People Respond to the Gospel

At its best, pastoral counseling seeks to use the insights and techniques of psychotherapy to help individuals and groups experience the unconditional love of God and to hear God's call for justice in all relationships.[33] The pastoral counselor makes use of the

---

[32]G. Lee Ramsey, Jr., personal correspondence.
[33]Cf. Charles V. Gerkin, *Introduction to Pastoral Care,* and Margaret Kornfeld, *Cultivating Wholeness: A Guide to Care and Counseling in Faith Communities* (New York: Continuum, 1998).

security of the counseling session and of the full range of counseling skills to help people sort out the various conscious and unconscious factors that prevent them from accepting God's unconditional love and acting on it.

Distress in the life of an individual, household, or small group affects the church as community. When persons and groups are limited in their receptivity to the gospel, they are often limited in the contribution they can make to the Christian witness. Consequently, pastoral counseling does more than heal individuals. It helps people experience and act on the gospel so that they can strengthen the witness of the community.

### *Christian Practices and Pastoral Counseling*

Christian practices often come into play in the counseling session. Indeed, counselors develop some of the practices to a high art–especially attentive listening, tolerating one another in failure, suffering with one another, providing hospitality, struggling to interpret the interlocking contexts within which the counselee lives from the perspective of the divine purposes for those contexts. Counseling sessions sometimes eventuate in the practices of prayer, confession of sin, and reconciliation.

Because pastoral counseling takes place in the Christian community, and because preaching interprets the life of the community, from time to time the sermon can help the congregation interpret what happens in pastoral counseling from a Christian perspective. The preacher can particularly help the congregation understand that pastoral counseling is not simply individual therapy but takes place for the sake of building up the community. Furthermore, the sermon can help the congregation realize that pastoral counseling takes account of the spiritual dimensions of the self and its relationships in a way that much secular counseling does not. The preacher can help the congregation understand how Christian practices come into play in pastoral counseling.

Most pastors have had minimal training in counseling. They know enough to help people with issues arising around typical life disturbances, such as matters of health, death, household issues, loss of employment, broken relationships. Additionally, pastors need to be sufficiently acquainted with diagnosis in counseling to identify problems that go beyond their training.[34] At these times, the pastor

---

[34]On diagnosis, see Nancy J. Ramsay, *Pastoral Diagnosis: A Resource for Ministries of Care and Counseling* (Philadelphia: Fortress Press, 1998), as well as Paul Pruyser's earlier *The Minister as Diagnostician: Personal Problems in Pastoral Perspective* (Philadelphia: The Westminster Press, 1976).

must be able to refer parishioners to professional counselors. For instance, few pastors are prepared to walk with parishioners in full-scale therapy in cases of abuse, incest, deep-seated marital conflict, or clinical depression. As G. Lee Ramsey, Jr., an authority on both pastoral counseling and preaching at Memphis Theological Seminary, points out, the pastor shows wisdom, humility, and courage by knowing when and how to refer.[35] An occasional sermon can help the congregation grasp this dimension of the minister's role in counseling.

## Preaching for a Community of Pastoral Care

Preaching has a pivotal place in the rediscovered role of pastoral care as a function of the congregational system. The sermon can alert the community to ways that pastoral care takes place through the life system of the congregation. The preacher can help the congregation name the formal, informal, and tacit ways that pastoral care takes place in the Christian community. The preacher can also contribute to pastoral counseling by helping shape the environment in which counseling takes place, and by helping the community reframe aspects of its understanding of pastoral counseling.

Perhaps the most important contribution that preaching can make to preventive pastoral care in our time is to help the congregation become a theological culture in which the congregation can consider situations of pastoral care. Another preventive function of preaching is to help the congregation enlarge its understanding of care to embrace the broad notion of care from historic Christian tradition. When Christians become conscious of the care that is taking place in their normal ecclesial worlds, the benefit of that care can multiply. For example, I listen more attentively to someone when I realize that listening attentively is a Christian practice that allows us not only to understand one another, to bond in a community of support, but also to know better how to serve God and one another.

Preachers can help the congregation prepare for major life disturbances by naming such disturbances, alerting people to the fact that such seasons of distress come to all of us, describing these situations, and exploring how the gospel helps us deal with them. Examples of situations that the preacher can bring into the purview of the congregation include death, illness, hospitalization, the changes in life that come with retirement and aging, living with mental and

---

[35]G. Lee Ramsey, Jr., personal correspondence.

physical challenges, divorce, adoption, loss of job. A preacher can help people in such circumstances, and others, accumulate resources to help them respond with the full resources of Christian faith. No amount of preparation is quite the same as experiencing difficulty, but resources can provide help.

One of the most significant things the preacher can do is to help the congregation understand the purpose and possibilities of healing care. The core of this task is to encourage the congregation to understand how God relates to the situation of difficulty, and to determine what they can expect from God and from the Christian community. Professor Black's distinction between cure and healing is liberating to many people.

The preacher can also help the congregation identify ways whereby care takes place throughout the life of the community, both formally and informally. The minister can encourage members to participate—as givers and receivers—in formal and informal means of support that are available through the church. Some people may not know about formal caregiving ministries or realize that they can be a part of them. Many people may not realize that they can both receive and mediate care through everyday relationships. When a major life disturbance happens to someone within the congregation or to the congregation as a whole, the preacher can devote a sermon to it.

Some Christians may think that they receive authentic pastoral care only from the minister. The sermon can expand the congregation's understanding of the priesthood of all believers by helping the congregation understand itself as a community of care.

The preacher can help the congregation recognize situations in which they can care for one another and for others. The preacher may introduce the community to basic skills that express care. However, the sermon is not an optimum setting for a workshop on skills for pastoral care. A preacher does not want to try to turn a congregation into amateur psychologists on the basis of a twenty-minute sermon. Nonetheless, a sermon can communicate valuable information.

Drawing on the historic understanding of pastoral care, the preacher may need to help the congregation recognize occasions when their faith and behavior disavow the gospel. The preacher may need to help the congregation understand that a statement such as, "No, our thoughts, actions, feelings, are not appropriate to the gospel," is an act of pastoral care. Such statements are designed to turn the flock away from patterns of mind, heart, and action that lead to destruction, and to turn it in directions that embrace the gospel. Clark M.

Williamson, Dean of Christian Theological Seminary, offers an analogy. A child with long hair is in the kitchen playing a game. The child is backing toward a gas stove with the front burner on high. As the child nears the stove, the parent sees that the long hair is in danger of catching on fire. The parent cries, "Stop!"

In the broad sense, healing pastoral care takes place when the Christian community criticizes and resists the principalities and the powers that corrupt the divine aims for human beings and for the world. These powers contribute to conditions that necessitate healing pastoral care when they create social pressures that distort the lives of human beings and of nature. Protesting injustice, for instance, is an act of pastoral care.

## Interactions of Pastoral Counseling and Preaching

Pastoral counseling can help the preacher. Counseling sessions can be a significant source of insight into the congregation's mind and heart. The questions and issues that surface in counseling an individual or a small group may reveal issues and anxieties that are shared by many in the congregation. The sermon can then offer a gospel interpretation of issues that come to expression in counseling. The congregation often participates in such sermons with unusual interest when they recognize that the preacher is dealing sensitively with issues that are important to them.

The pastor who brings insight from counseling into the pulpit must honor the confidentiality of the counseling session. A preacher is never free to refer to a specific case that the congregation might recognize unless the persons involved explicitly give their permission. If so, the preacher needs to tell the congregation that the persons involved in the case have given permission. A preacher who breaks confidentiality will find that the exposed parties feel that they have been treated unjustly. Trust erodes between the pastor and the congregation.[36]

### Overcoming Theological Amnesia

The pastoral counseling movement is revising several assumptions to help pastoral counseling serve the gospel more explicitly than in the therapeutic model discussed above.[37] Preaching can contribute

---

[36]Donald Capps, *Pastoral Counseling and Preaching*, 36–60, proposes that the tasks and movements of pastoral counseling can suggest the tasks and movement of occasional sermons.

[37]Charles V. Gerkin refers to the pastor as an "interpretive guide." See his *Widening the Horizons* and *Introduction to Pastoral Care*.

to this process. Pastoral counseling in the therapeutic paradigm sometimes suffers from theological amnesia. The counseling session often proceeds without explicit reference to the divine presence and its offers and requirements. A great gain of this emphasis is to free the counselee from the repressive authoritarianism sometimes found in religion.

However, this approach can make the self an idol. Creaturely desires become the ultimate measure by which to make life decisions. Furthermore, Christian theology often has great power to help interpret situations in which people find themselves. For instance, a woman who is in an abusive relationship may be surprised and liberated to find that Christian tradition regards abusive relationships as unjust.

Pastoral counselors in this mode sometimes reply that the counseling session embodies the gospel even when God is not explicitly named. The unconditional acceptance of the counselor is a means of communicating the unconditional acceptance of God. To be sure, God is present and working for the good of all, whether named or not. And the counselor certainly would not need to risk alienating the counselee by turning immediately and explicitly to religion. But when theological realities are introduced in a timely and sensitive way into a counseling relationship, they can often help people perceive the love and justice of God in liberating ways.[38]

The preacher can serve this dimension of pastoral counseling by helping the congregation develop a worldview with the gospel at its center. The sermon can help the congregation understand that many issues that lead to counseling have to do with religious dimensions of meaning. The preacher can help the congregation recognize that an adequate theological worldview can interpret the pain of life and point to healing. As appropriate, the sermon can call the congregation to repent.

When preaching nourishes a vision of God as unconditional love, people who come to counseling will often feel secure enough to deal with the deepest levels of the self. The sermon can help people understand the nature of divine power and the help that it provides. The sermon can particularly lead the congregation to recognize the character of the help that they can expect through counseling and through participation in the life of the community. When people come

---

[38]Cf. Browning, *The Moral Context of Pastoral Care;* John B. Cobb, Jr., *Theology and Pastoral Care* (Philadelphia: Fortress Press, 1977); William B. Oglesby, *Biblical Themes for Pastoral Care* (Nashville: Abingdon Press, 1980).

to counseling, they are then prepared to think about their situations from the perspective of the gospel.

## Transcending the Individualistic Understanding of Self

For many people in the therapeutic culture, self-fulfillment is measured by the degree to which one feels good about oneself and one's goals. The gospel calls us to transcend this autonomous understanding of selfhood. In Christian community, the self is the creation of a gracious God. God loves each person unconditionally and wills justice for all. In response, human beings are to love God and one another, and are to exercise justice in all relationships and situations.[39] Self-fulfillment, in a Christian sense, results from faithfully performing this task.[40]

Consequently, an increasing number of Christian counselors seek ways to help counselees take into account Christian values in connection with options for life that emerge in counseling.[41] Preaching can help with this dimension of pastoral care by encouraging the congregation to recognize distinctive boundaries between Christian and secular visions of human fulfillment. The preacher can articulate the gospel and explain that human fulfillment results from understanding oneself as loved unconditionally by God and by responding in trust and in living in accord with God's will for love and justice. The preacher can compare and contrast this view of self-fulfillment with other visions afloat in contemporary North American culture. Christians who enter counseling then (hopefully) bring with them a more distinctive Christian sense of self-fulfillment.

## Taking Account of Social Context

In the therapeutic paradigm, the counselor and counselee sometimes operate as if the individual were a self-enclosed entity. This way of thinking does not take sufficient account of the relationship between the social world of the congregation and the situation of the counselee. Indeed, Christian identity is communitarian. Social forces shape the world in which we live. These forces are economic, political, cultural, class, racial, ethnic, gender, philosophical, psychological,

---

[39]For provocative discussions of the relationship of therapeutic and liberation motifs, see Archie Smith, *The Relational Self: Ethics and Therapy from a Black Church Perspective* (Nashville: Abingdon Press, 1982) and Carroll A. Watkins Ali, *Survival and Liberation: Pastoral Theology in African American Context* (St. Louis: Chalice Press, 1999).

[40]Ironically, in the process, we often discover deeper senses of freedom, fulfillment, and feeling good about ourselves.

[41]E.g., Don S. Browning, *Religious Ethics and Pastoral Care,* Theology and Pastoral Care Series (Philadelphia: Fortress Press, 1983).

ecological, and religious.[42] Some forces promote a community of love and justice, while other forces undermine those very values.

We cannot accept a social determinism that sees human beings as only the products of systemic forces at work in our settings. Individuals can often decide a degree to which they are affected by their social worlds. Individuals and communities can become forces that shape social worlds. However, therapeutic counseling does not always help the counselee consider the effects of such forces on self and community.

Counseling in the therapeutic model often helps a person or a group cope with social forces. This kind of help is often essential as people struggle to survive from day to day. A counselor, for instance, may help a mother and children leave a home in which the dominant adult male regularly abuses them. However, counseling in the therapeutic pattern seldom leads people to critique or challenge the social forces that create the conditions that lead to the need for counseling. Ironically, by not helping people name and reject social forces that limit human life, therapeutic counseling enables those forces to continue to do damage. The counselor who provides unconditional positive regard for the counselee can prop up persons who lead social forces that wreak suffering. Such counseling can comfort cruel people to the end that they continue their cruelty.

Through sermons, the minister can engage in the Christian practice of helping the congregation understand the many interlocking contexts in which its members live. The congregation becomes aware of the dynamics of the social world within which their psychological lives take place. The preacher can help the congregation grasp connections between systemic social forces and their everyday lives that often lead parishioners to counseling. The preacher needs both to describe these contexts and to critique them from the standpoint of the gospel. In what ways do the social forces that affect us mediate God's love and call for justice? In what ways do these forces deny God's love or justice?

The preacher is further called to suggest ways by which the congregation can challenge such forces, and offer alternatives to them. In this latter context, the preacher and others in the congregation may engage in counseling for the purpose of strengthening members of the congregation to participate in refashioning the social world.

---

[42]On the interaction of persons and social systems from the standpoint of pastoral care, see Larry Kent Graham, *Care of Persons, Care of Worlds: A Psychosystems Approach to Pastoral Care and Counseling* (Louisville: Westminster/John Knox Press, 1992).

G. Lee Ramsey, Jr., rightly points out that a purpose of preaching is to help form the congregation as a community that can express pastoral care for the world.[43] The aim of pastoral care is ultimately not care of the community itself, but strengthening of the community for its witness in the world.

## Implications for Preachers

The church is now recovering a classical understanding by re-emphasizing that pastoral care focuses on strengthening the community so that it can express care for the world. Pastors continue to express pastoral care through individual counseling, but the counseling is designed to help people so that they can be more vital members of the community. Pastoral care, then, is not a particular function limited to individual or small-group therapy but is expressed throughout the congregational system.

Preaching is an act of pastoral care. The sermon is one way that the pastor exercises care for the community. The preacher helps build up the flock in the gospel. Most preachers who also engage in pastoral counseling do not regard individual therapy as an end in itself but as a means to building up the community and as a source of insight into the congregation. The preacher seeks to enhance the role of the sermon as an expression of care in the classical sense, and to work with other elements of the congregation to enhance the shepherding qualities of the congregational system. Among the most important roles of the preacher as pastoral caregiver are to

- help the congregation understand the emerging notion of a self as always a self-in-community, and a community that always includes God.

- help the community recognize the shift in emphasis in pastoral care from individual therapy to upbuilding persons for participation in community and witness. Indeed, therapy as conceived today is not just to help individuals develop good psychological health so that they can pursue their own goals, but is to help persons remove personal and social factors that impede their capacity to respond to and witness to God's love.

- help the congregation recognize how Christian practices function in individual counseling sessions.

---

[43]Ramsey, *Care-full Preaching*, 127–31.

- help the congregation realize that pastoral care takes place in Christian practices (e.g., listening attentively to one another) throughout the congregational system.

- function as preventive pastoral care by providing members of the community with important resources, especially theological, that can help the congregation struggle with fundamental life issues (e.g., identity, meaning, relationship, fulfillment as knowing and serving God, brokenness, sickness, death).

- be a form of healing pastoral care, especially with respect to issues that cause disequilibrium throughout the congregation.

- occasionally identify from the pulpit dysfunctional ways of behavior and how to correct them.

- model pastoral care by telling stories in sermons about people who care for one another in the full-bodied sense of the Bible and Christian tradition.

- be alert to points at which the sermon can reinforce (or correct) other forms of care in the congregational system. Likewise, the minister needs to be alert to points at which developments in other aspects of the congregation help the sermon express care, or call for the preacher to reconceive aspects of preaching in order to make sermons more caring.

- help the congregation ask of every event and relationship, "How does this event or relationship express pastoral care?"

- practice attentive listening to persons who come for counseling and discern some themes in the world of the congregation that can be addressed in preaching, as long as the preacher completely honors the confidentiality of the counseling relationship.

- engage in pastoral calling for its own sake. However, a preacher needs also to envision pastoral calling as a part of sermon preparation.

- help the congregation identify the relationship between systemic forces in the broader culture and difficulties facing individuals and small communities, and suggest actions by which the congregation can confront the principalities and powers as acts of pastoral care.

- help the congregation recognize that care is sometimes expressed through helping the congregation say no to thoughts, feelings, and behaviors that work against the gospel.

## Implications for the Theory of Pastoral Care

Pastoral counselors can support preachers by helping them recognize elements in the field of counseling that can assist them in analyzing the contexts within which they preach, and that can help them frame sermons. For instance, methods of pastoral diagnosis from counseling can sometimes help pastors understand phenomena in the congregation or in the world that the preacher can address in the sermon. Methods of reflection on the counseling session can sometimes be calibrated to the communal situation of the sermon. The preacher, of course, needs to be careful not to think of the sermon as individual counseling taking place in a corporate setting.

Preachers often deal with the life concerns of one or two groups in the congregation to the (often unconscious) neglect of others. Leaders in the field of pastoral counseling could also help preachers develop patterns of pastoral reflection that prompt them to consider all groups in the congregation. For instance, pastoral counselors could develop methods and materials to help pastors identify the various age groups in a congregation, their distinctive (and similar) life issues, and how to bring these concerns into preaching.

At one time or another, nearly all pastors preach a sermon that meets resistance in a congregation. However, the preaching community has developed few resources that even name this phenomenon, much less help preachers deal with it. Some resistance is active, but much is passive. Scholars in pastoral care could help preachers develop a better understanding of active and passive resistance, and could suggest specific ways whereby preachers could attempt to overcome resistance and create a better possibility for the congregation to receive the sermon.

Preaching, as a part of its contribution to the dimensions of the congregational system that express pastoral care, can remind caregivers to frame their care theologically. Pastoral counseling, in particular, often suffers from theological amnesia. As noted already, the counselor cannot move abruptly or insensitively to theological vocabulary and analysis in a counseling situation, but eventually a counselor in a Christian context wants to help counselees interpret their situation from the perspective of the gospel.

## Suggestions for Further Reading

Gerkin, Charles *Introduction to Pastoral Care.* Nashville: Abingdon Press, 1997. Places pastoral care in the context of social vision and community responsibility.

Miller-McLemore, Bonnie, and Brita Gill-Austern, eds., *Feminist and Womanist Pastoral Theology*. Nashville: Abingdon Press, 1999. Develops themes of care in and through community.

Ramsey, G. Lee, Jr. *Care-full Preaching: From Sermon to Caring Community*. St. Louis: Chalice Press, 2000. Develops ways in which preaching can develop the congregation as a community of care for the world.

Watkins Ali, Carroll A. *Survival and Liberation: Pastoral Theology in African American Context*. St. Louis: Chalice Press, 1999. Relates pastoral care to liberation theology with particular focus on the African American community.

# 4

# THE PREACHER AS ADMINISTRATOR

Many ministers today experience weariness. Most clergy are introverted personality types who expend tremendous energy exuding the extroversion required by ministerial encounters with other people. Furthermore, lack of role definition causes burnout as ministers try to do too many things with too little focus. Administration can aggravate this problem. Pastors who view themselves as chief executives can feel discouraged because they have too much to do in arenas in which they have little training or interest.

However, in the words of my colleague D. Bruce Roberts, "The day of administration as usual should be over."[1] Traditional church bureaucratic systems are seldom as effective as they were even a decade ago. Fresh approaches are needed.

Christian tradition and contemporary leadership theory point a way forward. The term *administrator* is derived from two Latin roots: *ad* ("to"), and *minister* ("serve"). An administrator serves the purpose of the church. Through the roles of administrator and preacher, the pastor can help a congregation discern its purposes and optimal ways

---

[1]D. Bruce Roberts, personal conversation.

to serve them. Preaching can play a pivotal role in helping the congregation reconceive leadership.

I first review how leadership functioned in the life systems of Israel and the early church. Then I consider possibilities for administration and preaching from Christian tradition, as well as from contemporary leadership theory. Finally, I explore ways that Christian practice and preaching can help shape administration.

## Traditions of Leadership

Discussion of leadership in the world of the Bible often takes place along a spectrum adapted from sociologist of religion Max Weber. According to Weber, leadership functions in community in two ways: as an expression of institutional authority to preserve the institution, or through charisma to reform the community.[2] However, scholars are increasingly dissatisfied with the simple dichotomy posed by institutional preservation versus charismatic reform. The actual exercise of leadership in the church is complex and reciprocal. The goal of leadership is to help the life system of the community serve God. Preaching plays a key role in these systems.

For much of the twentieth century, scholars interpreted the leadership of Israel in these ideal categories. Scholars considered priests representatives of established order. Charismatic prophets arose outside the establishment to protest corruption. Interpreters of early Christianity contrasted the charismatic impulse of the early church with the stiff bureaucracy of Israel. Scholars debated the degree to which the church was conflicted by anti-institutional flames and the drive toward mundane institutionalization.

However, when considering the major leaders and offices in Israel, Rodney Hutton, a scholar of the First Testament, noticed that institutional maintenance and charisma often interplay in the same person or office.[3] Yes, many persons and offices in Israel seek to preserve Israel. Yet many of these persons and offices are also open to change as required by fresh insights. The canonical picture of Moses, for instance, is neither simply an "embodiment of Israel's institutional forms" nor a figure of "unfettered charismatic power." Rather, "Moses

---

[2]Max Weber, *The Theory of Social and Economic Organization*, trans. A. M. Henderson and Talcott Parsons, ed. Talcott Parsons (Glencoe: The Free Press, 1947), 324–430. Weber distinguishes three ideal forms of authority: rational authority that depends upon formal legitimation, traditional authority that is legitimated by history and custom, and charismatic authority that is legitimated by extraordinary means.

[3]For a critical review, see Rodney L. Hutton, *Charisma and Authority in Israelite Society,* Overtures to Biblical Theology (Minneapolis: Fortress Press, 1994), 1–16.

symbolizes the force that is generated when power takes usable shape, when a bolt of electricity is directed into the high voltage line, when energy is transferred into physical form."[4] Hutton notes a similar confluence in the Bible's pictures of the judges, of the royal families, of the sages, and even of the priests and prophets.

The same is true in the early church. Kevin Giles, a pastor and professor of the Second Testament, finds a similar relationship between charismatic impulses and institutional interests in the leadership of the house churches, in the rise of the episcopate, and among deacons, elders, teachers, prophets, and apostles.[5] For instance, though leadership in Corinth was charismatic, it took institutional form (e.g., in early Christian prophets).

In both testaments, leadership is socially legitimated when it is consistent with the community's purpose, appropriate to the context, and exercised with pastoral sensitivity. Charismatic leadership is effective in a community only when the charismatic figure is perceived as being in tune with the community's guiding vision.[6]

The reciprocal relationship between maintenance of institutional order and charismatic innovation continues in church history. H. Richard Niebuhr and Daniel Day Williams notice the "astonishing adaptability and variety of the ministerial office along with the maintenance of its unity of purpose and dedication."[7] Clergy often take the lead both in preserving the stability of the church and in change. Clergy occasionally hoard power. Laity also perform these roles—sometimes in concert with clergy and sometimes in opposition. At its best, the church in history was a community of leadership.

After the close of the biblical period, increasingly complicated ecclesial structures appear. The priestly understanding of ministry came to the fore along with other forms of service (e.g., deaconesses, widows, acolytes, lectors, and exorcists). Leadership gradually becomes clergy-centered. Clergy exercise leadership by pronouncement, particularly through preaching. In Europe, the church was the major social structure to survive and give order to Europe after the collapse of Rome.

---

[4]Ibid., 42.

[5]Kevin Giles, *Patterns of Ministry Among the First Christians* (Melbourne: Collins Dove, 1989), passim.

[6]Bengt Holmberg, *Paul and Power: The Structure of Authority in the Primitive Church as Reflected in the Pauline Epistles* (Lund: Gleerup, 1978), 141–45.

[7]H. Richard Niebuhr and Daniel Day Williams, "Introduction," in *The Ministry in Historical Perspectives,* ed. H. Richard Niebuhr and Daniel Day Williams (New York: Harper & Brothers, 1956), viii.

However, the church did not become a static institution. Representing the interplay between institutional maintenance and charismatic innovation, the church adapted its structures to facilitate mission. The deacons, for instance, began to provide day-to-day care for the sick and the dying as well as adequate places of burial.[8]

By the sixteenth century, in the view of the Reformers, the church had lost sight of its gospel purpose and had become self-absorbed with ecclesiastical machinery. Clergy had become a separate caste within the church, often exercising authority arbitrarily.[9]

The Reformation was a charismatic impulse in the service of institutional renewal. The articulation of the priesthood of all believers was an innovative element in the Reformation's understanding of leadership. This doctrine holds that a congregation is a community of priests who mediate grace to one another. However, to ensure that essential elements of the gospel witness take place, the church sets aside some persons as ministers to represent the whole community.[10]

The community's decisions about the content of Christian faith, ethical behavior, and ecclesial structure are to emanate from the gospel. These principles come to expression with differing nuances. In some *Lutheran* congregations clergy had a dominant role, while in others the leading figures were princes, commissioners, or townspeople.[11] For *Calvin,* the minister exercised leadership first and foremost through teaching, especially through preaching. In Geneva, clergy and laity worked together in ecclesial leadership.[12] *Anglicans* sought to combine much of the structure of the Roman church with a component of community authorization typical of the continental Reformation. Churches in the *Wesleyan* movement, emphasizing education as a means of nurturing spiritual awareness, organized their local communities with an evangelical pragmatism. *Anabaptist* ecclesiology led to the most simplified pattern of leadership among churches descended from the Reformation. The work of the leader was largely to interpret the Bible.

In the churches descended from the Reformation, preaching is the *raison d'être* of leadership.[13] Preaching is part of a congregational

---

[8]George H. Williams, "The Ministry of the Ante-Nicene Church," in *The Ministry in Historical Perspectives,* 40.

[9]Ibid., 90–93.

[10]Wilhelm Pauck, "Ministry in the Time of the Continental Reformation," in *The Ministry in Historical Perspectives,* 111–13.

[11]Ibid., 122–25.

[12]Ibid., 126–31.

[13]Ibid., 131–35, esp. 135.

system that includes catechetical classes and home-to-home visitation.[14] The pastor's role is in dialectical relationship with the community. On the one hand, authority for leadership derives from having been set apart as community representative. On the other hand, the community "tests the spirits to see whether they are from God" (1 John 4:1).

In the United States, the combination of separation from Europe (with its landed churches) and the spirit of self-determination resulted in more clergy-lay sharing in leadership.[15] In this setting, the minister's leadership often depended as much on the informal relationship between the minister and the congregation as it did on ministerial office. Leadership was a function of the system of the congregation depending not only on formal polity but also on informal and tacit qualities in community.

Ronald Osborn describes twelve models of ministry that have been influential in North America (e.g., priest, awakener, pulpiteer, builder, impresario) and finds that the minister as manager is the most popular recent one.[16] This approach emerged in conjunction with the development of the managerial cohort in business. The structure of the church is parallel to a business. The minister is the manager of the church. The corporate executive and the minister employ similar management techniques.

Many theologically illiterate Christians measure the success of the church according to conventional statistical criteria typical of the North American success culture: membership, attendance, financial security, and influence in community. Many congregations turn to the wider culture for models of corporate management.[17] Furthermore, many clergy enjoy the feeling of self-importance that comes from partaking in the culture's image of the successful executive.[18]

To be sure, ministers need to be able to manage time and tasks and to work effectively with people. The church needs to pay some attention to its institutional health in order to be able to maintain its witness.

---

[14]Ibid., 136–38.

[15]Sidney E. Mead, "The Rise of the Evangelical Conception of Ministry in America (1607–1850)," in *The Ministry in Historical Perspectives,* 215–19. For Puritanism, see Winthrop S. Hudson, "The Ministry in the Puritan Age," in *The Ministry in Historical Perspectives,* 180–206.

[16]Ronald E. Osborn, *Creative Disarray: Models of Ministry in a Changing America* (St. Louis: Chalice Press, 1991), 137, 140.

[17]Ibid., 141–42.

[18]Ibid., 143.

However, the notion of management is deeply flawed as a comprehensive understanding of ministry.[19] The church is not an ecclesial corporation, but a theocracy. The success of the church cannot be measured in simple statistical terms, but by faithfulness. When management is a pastor's primary model for ministry, the pastor tends to take over more and more responsibility in the congregation. Members become passive and pastor-dependent, thus militating against the priesthood of all believers. A congregation and minister operating according to the managerial model are frequently prone to lose theological consciousness. Such a church asks people to work for the same reasons that the people work in other organizations. The notion of minister as manager does not stress the dimension of leadership that is most persistent in the Bible and Christian tradition: the call of the leader to help the church understand itself and the world in terms of the gospel and to become a community of leadership.

## Leadership and Community

The climate for leadership in the church is changing rapidly. The changes are significant in both the church's relationships to the larger culture and within the church.

For much of the nineteenth and twentieth centuries, the church in the United States was closely aligned with North American culture. The values of the culture were considered the values of the church, and vice versa. In this world, sometimes called Christendom, the culture fed new members to the church. The church was a not only a social force but high priest of the culture. In this ethos the minister could be an institutional caretaker who operated the established machinery of the church, which was organized like a corporation.[20] In some corners, Christian discipleship was correlated with the degree of participation in the institutional program of the church.

The sermon frequently had an institutional quality as the preacher exhorted the congregation to support church programs and to maintain social stability. Some preachers left the impression that to serve God was to serve the church. Although some clergy preached charismatically on subjects such as civil rights and the Vietnam war, analyses of sermons show that few preachers gave sustained attention

---

[19]Ibid., 145–48.
[20]Of course, in every generation the church has some charismatic pastors who are more than managers and caretakers.

to these matters. Most sermons focused on institutional maintenance or personal discipleship.[21]

This symbiotic relationship is ending. Increasingly, North Americans recognize that their culture is not a singular social world with commonly accepted values and religious assumptions, but is a pluralistic society of many communities with differing values. With pluralism comes relativism–the recognition that our perceptions are conditioned by our circumstances. No one person or community has a pure, absolute version of objective truth. All awareness is interpretive.[22]

The church can no longer assume that the culture will feed it new members or pay attention to its witness. Younger people commit themselves to the church only when they find that it adds meaning to their worlds. People outside the church pay positive attention to the Christian community only when its witness is relevant and intelligent. A church focusing on its own machinery is writing its own death certificate.

The institutional health of the historic denominations has also declined. Membership is shrinking. The church has fewer real dollars for ministry. The long-established churches have a smaller presence in the wider culture.

The reasons for this decline are many. The aforementioned breakdown of the informal alliance between church and culture removed the social obligation that propelled people to church. The birth rate in the long-established churches is low. Many congregations are located in regions with declining population. Congregations keep honest membership roles. Congregations in the historic denominations do not often have energetic membership recruitment, evangelistic emphases, or programming that attracts people today. These churches no longer stress tithing, and hence, frequently have feeble financial resources. Financial shortage heightens frustration.

However, the most important factor in the institutional diminishment of the historic churches is theological. Most people who leave these churches do so because the message of the church is not sufficiently compelling for them to invest themselves.[23] One of

[21]Cf. Ronald J. Allen, "What Are We Really Preaching?" *Pulpit Digest* 78/5 (1997): 78–85; cf. Buttrick, *A Captive Voice,* 9–10.

[22]Cf. Ronald J. Allen, Barbara Shires Blaisdell, and Scott Black Johnston, *Theology for Preaching: Authority, Truth, and Knowledge of God in a Postmodern Ethos* (Nashville: Abingdon Press, 1997).

[23]Clark Roof and William McKinney, *American Mainline Religion* (New Brunswick, N.J.: Rutgers University Press, 1987), 170.

my students was in a fieldwork assignment in a congregation of a historic denomination. She called on a thirty-something attorney who had drifted from the church who said, "Church just doesn't mean enough to me."

Preachers bear a share of responsibility for this situation. We have not sufficiently helped Christians understand the nature and claims of the gospel in comparison with the claims of other messages that vie for human loyalty today. We do not often preach with passion that ignites passion in others.

Two resources come together to help the church reconceive the pastor's administrative authority: the notion of the minister as leader as understood in the Bible and in Christian tradition, as well as fresh impulses in contemporary leadership theory. I now turn to these sources and their interaction.

## Teaching: The Pastor's Primary Administrative Responsibility

In the Bible and Christian tradition the call of the leader is to help the Christian community understand itself and the world in terms of the promise of God's unconditional love for each and all, and God's call for justice for each and all. The administrator is to help the community mobilize all aspects of its life to witness to the gospel in ways that fit its context.

When the community is healthy but in a settled and predictable situation, administration can have an institutional character (in Weber's terms). When the community is moribund, has drifted from its purpose, is out of step with its context, but exhibits possibility and creativity, administration needs to be more charismatic. Today's relationship of church and culture, as well as the theological and institutional malaise in many congregations, calls for a charismatic dimension.

The congregation does not set the minister aside to perform all its administration. Rather, the community calls the pastor to see that things happen that are essential to the community. The particular work of the minister is to teach the gospel.[24] Ronald Osborn notes that two of the most important contributions of the minister to the congregational system are theological vision and the motivation to embody that vision.[25]

---

[24]Cf. Wesner Fallow, *Church Education for Tomorrow* (Philadelphia: The Westminster Press, 1960); Edward Farley, *The Fragility of Knowledge* (Philadelphia: Fortress Press, 1988); Clark M. Williamson and Ronald J. Allen, *The Teaching Minister* (Louisville: Westminster/John Knox Press, 1991).

[25]Osborn, *Creative Disarray,* 46–47.

A major part of the administrative task of the minister is to help the community grasp these roles of community and pastor. Preaching can be a great help.

Next to helping the congregation remember who it is and what it is to do, the pastor's most important administrative task is to try to create an atmosphere in which all persons can identify, prepare for, and exercise the contributions they can make to the leadership of the community.

Helping a congregation become this kind of congregation is a long-term project. I have frequently been in planning meetings in which the person presiding attempts to create an environment in which the group can create a program from its own resources. The chair, seeking to avoid manipulation and to encourage the community leadership, says, "What would you like to do?" After an awkward silence, the people contribute ideas that they have encountered at the Optimist Club, the neighborhood block party, or while reading *Redbook*. The group seldom asks how its ideas cohere with the purpose of the church. The discussion is often a mirror of trends from the surrounding culture.

From the standpoint of systems thinking, one of the first tasks of the pastor as administrator is to locate groups and persons in the congregation who are influential in the congregational system and to help them rediscover the heart of Christian faith and the notion of the congregation as a community of leadership. In formal terms, who within the church most needs to consider these perspectives? For example, which leadership bodies most shape the life of the congregation? Informally, who are people and groups whose place in the life system can enhance (or frustrate) the formation of the congregation?

## Administrative Renewal

New motifs in leadership theory can help a congregation recreate aspects of its organizational life in ways that honor the gospel, the changing contexts of the church, and the role of the minister as teacher. Acting in a charismatic mode, the congregation needs to think together about promising options. Edgar Schein uses the popular image of creating a culture as an overarching image for administration.[26] Church leaders try to develop the congregation as a culture informed by the gospel.

---

[26]Edgar H. Schein, *Organizational Culture and Leadership,* 2d ed. (San Francisco: Jossey-Bass, 1992).

Margaret Wheatley finds clues for changing patterns of leadership in the "new science" represented by quantum physics, self-organizing systems, and chaos theory.[27] Newtonian physics, speaking for the "old science," views the universe as a machine in which each part has certain functions. When the parts function as they are designed, the machine makes the product envisioned by those who designed it and turned it on.

Many congregations are Newtonian in organization. Year after year, leaders operate the same congregational machinery in much the same way, hoping they will get satisfactory results. When aspects of congregational life languish, leaders work harder.

Such management styles are behavior-centered. Management decisions are made by persons in the upper reaches of the hierarchy and are implemented in a linear sequence, flowing from executives to supervisors to workers. This model assumes that those on the higher end of the management scale possess the perspective to make decisions of maximum benefit for the institution. Such utilitarian management focuses on motivating external behavior.

Managers in the church sometimes take this approach. We try to get the machine to produce the desired behavior. For example, we try to get people to serve on committees. We seek to get people to contribute to the financial drive. The number of people who serve and the amount of money pledged gauge the success of leadership.

Cutting edge thinkers about leadership today replace these Newtonian approaches with ones that are in harmony with the "new science." The new science views the universe not as a machine but as a living organism, a system of relationships in which all things are interconnected even when those connections are unseen. When elements of the universe come together in fresh configurations, creative developments can occur.[28] Administration tries to help the congregation envision itself as a community of relationships.

Self-organizing systems in nature and in social settings organize themselves in response to their environments. Groups that are open to influences from outside often find that they can take advantage of new opportunities. Changes within a natural setting or a group can have an effect on the natural or social environment.[29]

---

[27]Margaret J. Wheatley, *Leadership and the New Science: Learning About Organization from an Orderly Universe* (San Francisco: Berrett-Koehler Publishers, 1994).

[28]Wheatley, *Leadership and the New Science*, 25–74.

[29]Ibid., 75–120.

The thinking of the new science is particularly striking in regard to chaos. Whereas disorder and chaos threaten Newtonians, chaos theory sees disorder as creating conditions that can birth new possibilities. Disruption can be frightening, but it can be an important step in helping a community clarify its purposes and behavior.[30]

Some writers use the term *synergy* to describe this phenomenon. In a synergistic process, the whole that results is greater than the sum of its parts.[31] From this point of view, administration brings people together to generate new possibilities for community life. Administration helps a community think in a new science way about its self-ordering. Good administration provides support that allows a community to make its way through chaos in the realization that disruption can be a prelude to new life.

When applied to congregational administration, this synergistic model suggests that the congregation should not assume that it needs to maintain old forms of congregational life, especially when those forms frustrate the mission of the community. Congregational administrators need to bring the community together to envision ways of structuring congregational life that take account of the present context of the congregation and the synergy of persons in the current generation.

Using this model, I know a congregation of 110 members who were weary from staffing a massive, traditional committee structure that dated from the days when the congregation had a membership of 1,000. One year, the newly elected moderator of the congregation could not get persons to chair even half the committees. In a synergistic moment, the congregation scrapped the traditional committee structure in favor of task forces to coordinate church life according to the seasons of the church year. The church now has a group to co-ordinate Advent and Christmas, another for Lent, one for Easter and Pentecost, and multiple groups for Ordinary Time. People in leadership now feel less that they are staffing a bureaucracy and more that they are shaping the life of a dynamic community.

In an even newer and bolder approach, a congregation might adopt "a zero-based approach" to church organization. This notion is adapted from the process of preparing budgets used in business a few years ago. When preparing an annual budget, an organization typically begins with categories inherited from the previous year, and

---

[30]Ibid., 121–38.
[31]Stephen R. Covey, *The Seven Habits of Highly Effective People: Restoring the Character Ethic* (New York: Simon and Schuster Publishing Co., 1989), 262–84.

then determines how much money is needed in each category for the next year. By contrast, zero-based budgeting begins at ground zero by asking, What is our purpose? What do we need to fund to give us the best opportunities to fulfill our purpose? Planners take nothing for granted. A zero-based budget may contain new categories. If a group within the organization no longer serves the purpose of the organization in an optimum way, that group is not funded. The whole organization may be reconceived or shut down.

When suggesting that a congregation take a zero-based approach to its life, I am thinking of more than zero-based budgeting. A congregation can begin at ground zero in all its thinking about the organization that a church needs today. The community imagines as many ways as possible that the future church might organize to fulfill its purpose. Eventually, the church must select options that seem most promising, but, initially, no possibility is summarily given imperial status or rejected.

Zero-based thinking begins by not *assuming* that the congregation in its *current form* is the optimum mode of expression for Christian community. To be sure, local communities need to have some structure to enact Christian witness. But there is no inherent reason why we should think that the congregation must always exist on the present highly institutional model.

The life of the typical congregation mirrors many businesses and civic entities in North America. We have a constitution and bylaws that create a corporate structure with a board of directors and committees ad infinitum. We own a building. We pay staff. We recruit new members. We run the same annual program. Zero-based thinking begins by asking, What are the *essential* elements for Christian life? How can we best create a community that gives itself wholly to that mission? Congregations that emerge from zero-based processes could be quite different. They might not all have buildings, or boards, or membership rolls, or even (gasp) paid clergy. They might be more like the house churches of the first century than like today's civic institutions.

A caveat. Decisions reached in these contexts will not always result in bold departures from the past. New configurations of people in new situations may discover that familiar organizational patterns are fine institutional carriers for the future.

## Synergism and Christian Practice

The rediscovery of Christian practice in our time is happening in the way just described. Christian community is rediscovering potential in these practices. Although quite old, their use in the contemporary church often quickens those who practice them. Indeed, contemporary culture's stress on the new and the novel leaves some people feeling orphaned from other communities, times, and places. Engaging in practices with roots in antiquity helps many people feel an empowering sense of tradition.

This approach to administration requires administrators who are comfortable with not controlling group process, who can help the community implement fresh patterns of life, and who can lead a community in thinking critically about ideas that emanate from its life. It requires administrators and community members who can live with uncertainty as group life is in process.

Synergistic processes depend on several Christian practices. Members of the community struggle together to interpret the many interlocking contexts of the congregation. Persons in this mode of relationship must listen attentively to one another. The members of the community are attempting to work together to maintain the social structure of the congregation to sustain its witness, so that it can work together with other communities to maintain the life of the wider society. In the broad sense, a congregation in the midst of synergizing possibilities for its life needs to be hospitable toward persons, communities, and ideas outside its typical purview. Hitherto unfamiliar communities and ideas may contain seeds for renewal.

Fresh impulses in contemporary leadership philosophy contribute to the renewal of church administration. Stephen Covey, a dynamic thinker in this field, summarizes these impulses. Administration has less to do with management techniques than with developing a community ethos in which people relate to one another with trust and work together toward a common mission. According to Covey, the first aim of leadership is to help shape character, that is, to help persons own the core values of the organization.[32] Character-centered leaders seek ways to help members of the community strengthen hearts that resonate with the values of the institution so that outward behavior becomes an expression of inward conviction. Lasting institutional change occurs as people are transformed in heart and mind. Such persons do not simply perform tasks but become personal and communal embodiments of the purposes of the organization.

Robert Greenleaf pioneers the servant leader as paradigm of administration.

[32]Covey, *The Seven Habits of Highly Effective People,* 18–23.

The servant leader is a servant first...[Servant leadership] begins with the natural feeling that one wants to serve, to serve *first*...The difference [between servant leadership and other forms of leadership] manifests itself in the care taken by the servant–first to make sure that other people's high priority needs are being served. The best test, and the most difficult to administer, is: Do those served grow as persons? Do they, *while being served*, become healthier, wiser, freer, more autonomous, more likely themselves to become servants? *And*, what is the effect on the least privileged in society? Will they benefit, or at least, not be further deprived?[33]

The servant leader serves the community by helping the community serve its purpose.

## A Clear Mission

Another contribution of contemporary philosophy of leadership is the emphasis that vital organizations have a clear sense of mission. They can distinguish attitudes and actions that are central to the organization from those that are secondary. Empowered by a forceful understanding of purpose, a community can nurture things that enhance its mission and turn away from things that distract it.

Consequently, many contemporary leadership theorists encourage communities to write mission statements that summarize the purpose of the community.[34] For instance, University Park Christian Church (Disciples of Christ) in Indianapolis, the congregation of which I am part, states its mission: "University Park Christian Church is called by God to be a reconciling community in our broken and fragmented world, witnessing to God's healing and transforming love that we know through Jesus." The notion of reconciliation is key. A purpose of the congregation is to announce human reconciliation with God as confirmed through Jesus Christ. This congregation also understands its purpose to include reconciliation within the human community. University Park, a predominately European American congregation, jointly owns its building with the predominately African American Faith United Christian Church

---

[33]Robert K. Greenleaf, *The Servant as Leader* (Indianapolis: Robert K. Greenleaf Center for Servant-Leadership, 1991), 7; cf. Robert K. Greenleaf, *Servant Leadership: A Journey into the Nature of Legitimate Power and Greatness* (New York: Paulist Press, 1977).

[34]E.g., Covey, *The Seven Habits of Highly Effective People*, 95–144; Peter M. Senge, *The Fifth Discipline: The Art and Practice of the Learning Organization* (New York: Doubleday Currency, 1990), 1.

(Disciples of Christ). University Park understands its mission to include encouraging reconciliation among the races, and among other arbitrary divisions of the human family.

However, having a mission statement will not automatically impart a sense of identity and power for mission in a community. Mission statements that are most deeply embraced by a community typically arise from the people themselves and are not imposed by the hierarchy. Processes that take advantage of synergism often generate mission statements that empower many people in the community.

Given that the circumstances of an organization change, and that new combinations of people call forth fresh patterns of relationship and energy and activity, a mission statement is more a marker on the road than an end. Indeed, "Today's problems [may] come from yesterday's 'solutions.'"[35] An organization needs to revisit the mission statement regularly to determine the adequacy of the statement from the standpoint of the community's present context and constancy.

Many congregations have generated mission statements in the last decade. However, these statements seldom result in revitalization. My impression is that the theological illiteracy of many congregations plays an informal role in undermining the effect of the statements. The mission is sometimes stated in theological language that the congregation does not fully grasp. Some mission statements are the work of a small group, rather than the congregation as a whole. Many congregational mission statements are so general that they do not help the congregation have well-defined priorities. Many mission statements disappear from congregational life after they are written.

Peter Senge, a leading thinker about leadership and community, uses the term "learning organization" to describe an essential quality of communal life. A learning organization is one "where people continually expand their capacity to create the results they truly desire, where new and expansive patterns of thinking are nurtured, where collective aspiration is set free, and where people are continually learning how to learn together."[36] Making use of attentive listening, a learning organization learns about itself from as many sources as possible, and adapts its life to account for what it learns.

Writing in a similar vein of "the learning congregation," Thomas Hawkins notes that everyone in the community is responsible for the learning that takes place. "Yet something that is everyone's

---

[35]Senge, *The Fifth Discipline,* 57.
[36]Ibid., 1.

responsibility runs the risk of becoming no one's responsibility."[37]
The preacher can help the congregation become a responsible
learning organization.

Today's literature in leadership stresses that communities need
to have an experimental attitude in organizational life. Changes in
institutional life, especially in the first months and years of a revision,
are viewed less as permanent strategies, and more as experiments.
The leader's success is not measured as much in conventional
quantifiable terms as on the basis of the degree to which organizational
experiments help the institution learn.

Christian communities are encouraged to reflect on their current
situations and organizational innovations from the perspectives of
appropriateness to the gospel, intelligibility, and moral plausibility.
The community then adapts this part of its life in order to build on
the strengths and to strengthen the weaknesses.

This experimental attitude is particularly needed in the church.
For much of the last half of the twentieth century, congregational life
followed linear organizational patterns that imitated similar patterns
in business. These approaches called for massive mechanisms of
congregational governance and large numbers of people involved in
committees. Many people today are wearied by maintaining church
machinery, but are eager for relationship and for participation that
adds value to life. Hence, one of the most important administrative
actions of a pastor or congregational council is to gather people in
synergistic settings to imagine fresh approaches to congregational life.
Preaching can help create this synergistic field.

## Preaching as Administration

The emphasis of preaching moves back and forth between
institutional maintenance and charismatic renewal. The preacher must
read the signs of the times in the congregation to determine the
interplay between them.

According to the Bible, Christian tradition, and contemporary
leadership theory, the indispensable contribution the preacher makes
to the administration of the congregation is to help the community
understand the gospel as the heart of its life. The gospel bestows
identity and calls forth witness. The organization of the congregation
is vacuous without an animating theological charter. From this point

---

[37]Thomas R. Hawkins, *The Learning Congregation: A New Vision of Leadership* (Louisville: Westminster John Knox Press, 1997), 49.

of view, the sermon is one of the most important administrative acts of the minister. In Steven Covey's language, the sermon is a primary means for forming the character of the congregation.

The preacher can help the congregation see the two sides of the collapse of Christendom. On the one hand, the church can no longer count on the culture for a steady stream of new members and automatic influence within the wider culture. We need to find fresh ways of evangelizing, recruiting members, and supporting the institution. On the other hand, the changed situation is a time of great adventure for the church. Today's clergy and congregational leaders are not simply caretakers of an institution. Moreover, the disestablishment of the church may mean that the congregation can free itself from some of the ways in which the church has been co-opted by the culture. If the culture is not writing the check to support the church, the church may witness more prophetically.

This preaching task includes helping the congregation understand the distinctiveness of the church as a community. To carry out its vocation, the church needs to know the content of its calling. The preacher needs to help the community understand that faithfulness to the gospel is the norm by which to measure the success of the church.

Ministers often feel pressure—from within themselves as well as from the congregation—for the institutional programs of the church to succeed in conventional statistical terms. Hence, ministers often use the sermon to advertise church programs and to recruit people for them. Some sermons nag, lobby, or bully. However, this approach works against the purpose for which they are intended. It reduces the pulpit to an advertising medium. It communicates that the success of the church is gauged by the same standards by which we evaluate businesses and volunteer organizations. It may hint that service to God is primarily service to the church. Such sermons can be self-serving for both the church and the preacher. When people feel manipulated or bullied, their receptivity to the message plummets.

Of course, occasions arise in the congregation when the preacher needs to lead the congregation in a significant conversation about aspects of its life. For instance, a preacher might want to help a congregation reflect on factors going into a decision on whether or not to build a community center on the back lot of the church property.

Ministers often want the congregation to be more energized. However, the most reliable way to increase energy in a congregation is not to exhort people to greater activity, but to help the congregation catch the vision of the glory of God. The focus should be theological.

The sermon can help the congregation understand that the organizational life of the church has changed frequently in history. Many congregations assume that present church life is the way it has always been. The awareness of change in the past can help congregations be open to the possibility of change in the present.

The preacher needs to help the congregation understand the change in perception that accompanies the transition from the "old science" to the "new science" thinking about organizations. This conceptual framework will help congregations who need to be open to fresh patterns of congregational life.

The preacher can introduce the congregation to the notions of synergism and zero-based approaches to leadership. Beyond providing basic information, the sermon can help the congregation in one of two ways: (1) To persons who are accustomed to fixed patterns of institutional life, post-Newtonian administration can be unsettling. Hence, the sermon can sometimes serve the gospel by providing the assurance of the divine presence in the process of creativity. (2) However, at times, the sermon itself may need to be a force that helps destabilize the community so that fresh possibilities for the congregation are allowed to emerge. The preacher may be called to be an agent of chaos in an otherwise stable situation so that the congregation can be liberated from suffocating stability.

The pastor should regularly preach on the meaning of the mission statement and its implications. Indeed, the minister might put together a sermon, or series of sermons, that interprets the mission statement. The preacher can help the church recognize how the mission statement leads the congregation to make decisions about how to invest its time and other resources. Furthermore, as we have noted, current literature in Christian practice suggests that when a community engages in a practice repeatedly, the content of the practice eventually begins to contribute to the formation of the community. Toward this end the congregation might regularly speak aloud the mission statement in worship and in other settings in the congregation (e.g., at meetings of governing bodies).

The preacher can help the congregation understand the reasons for innovations in church life by identifying problems in former patterns and improvements in church life sought in the innovations. However, experiments sometimes fail. This will happen as the church tries new forms of ecclesial life. At such times, the preacher can help the congregation practice tolerating one another in failure, and perhaps even to confess ways in which their sin is complicit in failure.

The preacher can explain the notion of the congregation as a learning organization and can alert the congregation to arenas in which it can learn. Indeed, the sermon itself can be a significant event of learning.

In the spirit of the learning organization, preachers need to seek feedback on their preaching from the congregation and from persons in the wider world of preaching. Feedback allows preachers to build on strengths of patterns of communication, and to seek to improve aspects of communication that are sometimes clouded.

The preacher can encourage an experimental attitude in the congregation. People are especially responsive to stories of experiments from other congregations.

In all these things, however, the preacher needs to honor the fundamental work of the pulpit. The preacher is to help the congregation reflect on the degree to which all aspects of its life are appropriate to the gospel, intelligible, and morally plausible. In the headiness and frightfulness of innovation, preachers and congregations can easily lose sight of that simple but essential task.

Duties associated with a chief operating officer eat into time that the minister needs to give to preparation for preaching. Other tasks often seem to have a more immediate claim on the minister's time—returning phone calls, drawing an organizational chart needed for tonight's meeting, helping the crew from the heating and cooling company find the furnace. Preachers can draw on the doctrine of the priesthood of all believers to rectify this situation.

By virtue of theological education, ministers tend to be better equipped than most other members of the community for enlarging Christian mind, heart, and will. Ministers tend not to be so well equipped for other aspects of leadership. Other members are often much more skilled than clergy at running meetings, fund-raising, working with the budget, recruiting and supporting volunteers, dealing with the machinations of committees, caring for property, ordering supplies, enrolling young people for camp, supervising the Habitat for Humanity house, or leading a rally against the death penalty.

The preacher can help the congregation actualize the priesthood of all believers so that the gifts of the congregation are coordinated with the needs of the body. The preacher can thus be freed from the wear of daily supervision of the congregation and can focus on preparation for preaching and teaching.

When I was ordained, I thought that to be a good administrator, I largely needed a daytimer, a calendar, skill at planning, and the discipline to carry out basic tasks, such as returning phone calls and recruiting. This chapter reveals the inadequacy of that vision. However, I close with these motifs because they can be a great help to the preacher when adapted to the revised notion of administration.

A pastor often finds it helpful to use a daytimer to identify the tasks that need to be done each day and to prioritize. A daytimer can help the preacher set aside the times of the day that are most fruitful for sermon preparation. Preaching textbooks frequently admonish a pastor to set aside the first two hours of the day for sermon preparation. Lock the study door. Turn off the phone. However, some preachers are more creative at other times. Some preachers work best in large blocks; they devote two afternoons or even a day for preparation. Preachers need to find and use their optimum times.

I sometimes hear ministers say, "I don't have time for sermon preparation until late in the week." The early part of the week is consumed by office work, meetings concerning church programs, and (for the better pastors) pastoral calling. Sermon preparation gets pushed to Friday, Saturday, or even Sunday morning.

To this situation I reply with a question and two statements. The question: How can you not make time to prepare for your part in the largest regular gathering of the congregation–the public worship of God? The statements: A proper sense of ministerial priorities will help you prune many time- and energy-consuming activities from your schedule and put them in the hands of laity (who, in these areas, may actually be more capable than you), leaving you with sustained time for sermon preparation. A daytimer can help you organize the components of your day

An annual calendar alerts the pastor to upcoming events. Such a calendar can help the preacher identify things that will happen in the congregation (and in the larger world) that call for homiletical attention. A pastor can also chart times throughout the year to pause and reflect critically on the degree to which the gospel is the generative force in the life of the congregation. Many preachers now work in colleague groups on the interpretation of Bible passages from the Revised Common Lectionary.

Retreats and other events can generate ideas that can become a part of the life of the congregation. Many preachers find it helpful to take periodic retreats to plan their preaching for a season. Such planning means that the minister is not living from hand to mouth. Ministers often find that they need to leave the office to have uninterrupted time. A number of preachers take sermon-planning retreats together at a church camp, state park, conference center, private cabin, or motel.

## Implications for Preachers

The heart of administration or leadership is not tending to the details of institutional mechanics (though that is important), but is helping the community articulate its vision and organize and mobilize its life so as to enact that vision. The minister as administrator is usually less the charismatic visionary and organizer who must personally perform all administrative responsibilities, but is more a presence in the congregation who seeks to empower the community itself toward these tasks. The sermon's most important administrative role is to help the congregation interpret the vision of the community and its patterns of organization from the perspective of the gospel. The sermon can contribute to the administrative life of the congregation in several important ways:

- Help the community embrace the gospel as the raison d'être of the congregation. The preacher can particularly help the congregation recollect the specific implications of its own mission statement for the congregational system.

- Help the community recognize the shift in emphasis taking place today in congregational leadership from thinking of the minister as the chief executive of the congregation to thinking of the congregation as a community of responsible parties and leaders.

- Reflect on the congregation's patterns of communal life, such as its organizational structure patterns of relationship. However, the preacher does not want to turn to these matters so often as to leave the impression that the sermon, and the church, are institutionally preoccupied.

- Help the congregation realize that the church is in a period of transition, that the stable and heavily bureaucratic congregational life characteristic of the last century is giving way to more relational, purpose-driven patterns of Christian community. The minister can help the congregation recognize that it is in an experimental time in these regards.

- Assure the congregation of the divine presence in the midst of creativity.

- Create enough disequilibrium in the congregation to provoke an awareness of the need to think afresh regarding the community's mission and organization.

- Seek feedback from parishioners on the preaching. What does the minister learn from such feedback that reinforces current patterns of preaching or that calls for change?

- Help the congregation ask of every document, meeting, event, and organization in the congregation, How does this event or group express the mission of the congregation?

The preacher can help the congregation recognize how Christian practices come into play in the administrative life of the congregation. This means that the preacher needs to:

- show the congregation how to tolerate each other in failure.

- determine the best times of day and/or week for sermon preparation, and make him- or herself available for that task at that time;

- benefit from planning of sermons (at least in a general way) a long time in advance; and

- keep the congregation informed about the pastor's own ministry and time commitments.

## Implications for Theories of Administration

While the trend toward lay participation in leadership is a move in the direction of actualizing the priesthood of all believers, it requires a laity that is theologically literate. Unfortunately, as already noted, theological illiteracy is commonplace in congregations in the long-established denominations. Preachers need to urge authorities in the field of leadership to stress that developing a theologically mature congregation is foundational to the church's becoming a synergistic community of leadership. Otherwise, the church's synergism is likely to be nothing other than a reshuffling of prevailing attitudes, behaviors, and organizational purposes imported from the culture.

One of the key elements of a learning organization is reflecting on its own life, learning from others, and making changes accordingly. Receiving feedback is often an important component of this process. By contrast, preachers receive very little feedback other than the comments people make at the door, occasional conversations about the preaching by the pastoral support committee (or some other church body), remarks that people make about the preaching in informal settings, and attitudes and actions that arise in the congregation that suggest the influence of preaching. Leaders in the field of leadership could help pastors develop both formal and informal ways of receiving and interpreting feedback on their preaching. Such help might include survey instruments that preachers could use, methods of interviewing groups and individuals. This assistance might also include helping preachers develop the skill of listening for the effects of preaching among parishioners in settings far removed from the preaching event or from providing feedback. Given the importance of change in the contemporary church, leaders in administration could develop materials on how sermons can help facilitate systemic change in a congregation. Such direct guidance for preaching, of course, should be in the context of larger processes of change. How do administrators introduce ideas for change? How are such ideas nurtured and with whom? What can the preacher do as a part of the congregation's systemic consideration of the possibility of change?

Preaching can remind persons thinking about administration and leadership in the church of the necessity of thinking of leadership from the perspective of the gospel. Regardless of how helpful principles of the new science or the theory of the learning organization can be to the church, they do not provide sufficient criteria against which to evaluate the life of the Christian community. Leadership theory itself should be measured by the criterion of appropriateness to the gospel.

## Suggestions for Further Reading

Covey, Steven R. *The Seven Habits of Highly Effective People: Restoring the Character Ethic* (New York: Simon and Schuster, 1989). Emphasizes the development of character as the leader's most important task.

Greenleaf, Robert K. *Servant Leadership: A Journey Into the Nature of Legitimate Power and Greatness* (New York: Paulist Press, 1977). Images the leader as servant not only of organizational purposes but also of the greater good of persons and human family.

Hawkins, Thomas R. *The Learning Congregation: A New Vision of Leadership* (Louisville: Westminster John Knox Press, 1997). Envisions the congregation as a community of leadership through learning, especially reflecting on, and learning from, their own experience.

Senge, Peter M. The *Fifth Discipline: The Art and Practice of the Learning Organization* (New York: Doubleday Currency, 1990). Calls organizations to reflect on their patterns of life and to learn from them, making change as necessary.

Wheatley, Margaret J. *Leadership and the New Science: Learning about Organizations from an Orderly Universe* (San Francisco: Berrett-Koehler Publishers, 1994). Applies the "new science" to organizations.

# 5

# THE PREACHER AS MISSIONARY

I once heard someone say that mission is to the church as burning is to fire. A fire is a fire when it is aflame. Before a fire starts to burn, it is potentially a fire. After flames die, they are no longer a fire. When a fire stops, we see its effects–ashes, charred wood, metal twisted by heat–but fire is burning. So it is with the church and mission.

A change of focus is underway. Christian leaders sometimes consider mission as an activity of the church alongside other activities. For instance, congregations organized by committees often think of mission as a function of the world outreach committee. To support these activities, the pastor occasionally preaches on social action or world outreach. However, leaders in thinking about mission (a discipline sometimes called missiology) today stress that mission is not a function of but the essence of the church. The church *is* mission. From this perspective, preaching both interprets mission and is itself an expression of mission.

This chapter first overviews how the Bible and Christian tradition understand mission, and the roles preaching has played in mission. I articulate a brief theology of mission and ruminate on preaching as mission. I relate these perspectives to three expressions of mission: evangelism, quest for social justice, and all that Christians do. The chapter considers preaching as mission. Along the way, it explores how Christian practices are integral to understanding and embodying mission.

## Mission in the Bible and in Christian Tradition

The mission of the church derives from the mission of God in the world, the *missio dei*.[1] The *missio dei* is to lead the world, now broken and twisted by sin, to become a cosmic community of love and justice.[2] God's mission is not just to build up the church, but is for every person, community, and situation to embody these divine purposes. The church is called to participate in the *missio dei* by witnessing to God's unconditional love for all and God's unrelenting call for justice for all.[3]

## *The Reign of God*

Genesis 1 states the *missio dei.* This poem depicts the world as a cosmic life system as God intends–a vast community in which all elements relate together in mutual support. This passage is also the foundation of the biblical notion of justice; justice is relationships that mirror those of the world at creation. Injustice occurs when people and nature do not live in such covenantal community.

The story of the fall (Genesis 3) explains why the world is not now the way God planned. The world is broken–an arena of sin, alienation, poverty, sickness, suffering, violence, and death. The rest of the Bible tells of ways that God seeks to restore the world to an Edenic quality. Initially, God works with the whole human race (Genesis 4:1–11:32). When this attempt fails, God works with one human family (Genesis 12:1ff).

---

[1]David J. Bosch, *Transforming Mission: Paradigm Shifts in Theology of Mission* (Maryknoll: Orbis Books, 1991), 389–93; Lesslie Newbigin, *The Open Secret: An Intro-duction to the Theology of Mission,* rev. ed. (Grand Rapids: Wm. B. Eerdmans, 1995) and his *Mission in Christ's Way: Bible Studies,* WCC Mission Series (Geneva: World Council of Churches, 1987).

[2]Cf. Donald Senior, C.P., and Carroll Stuhlmueller, C.P., *The Biblical Foundations of Mission* (Maryknoll: Orbis Books, 1983).

[3]See Clark M. Williamson and Ronald J. Allen, *The Vital Church: Teaching, Wor-ship, Community Service* (St. Louis: Chalice Press, 1997), 25–47. The viewpoint in this chapter is consistent with a shift that has taken place in the World Council of Churches in understanding God's relationship with the church and the world. Through much of the twentieth century, this relationship was conceived as God moving through the church to the world. However, since the 1960s, the Council has increasingly viewed God as moving through the world with the church as witness to God's movement. See Priscilla Pope-Levison, "Evangelism in the WCC," *International Review of Mission* (1991): 233–34.

The mission of God through Israel is clear: "I will make of you a great nation, and I will bless you, and make your name great, *so that* you will be a blessing...in you all the families of the earth shall be blessed" (Genesis 12:2–3).[4] God elects Israel so that Israel's life system can model for other peoples the ways of God that bless. This theme runs through much of the literature in the First Testament. Through Isaiah, for instance, God says, "I have given you as a covenant to the people, a light to the nations" (42:6).

Priests, prophets, and sages all preach. While their sermons have different nuances according to their theological interests, they share the common task of helping the congregation discover the mission of God. The prophets, for instance, alert the community to points at which they need to correct imbalances in faith or ethical behavior.

From Abraham and Sarah (circa 2000 B.C.E.) through the Hellenistic Age (circa 200 C.E.), Israel fulfills its mission by living among other peoples. The nations are supposed to be able to see the way of blessing by observing Israel's life system.

Most of the early Christian communities were influenced by apocalypticism. This theological point of view holds that history is divided into periods: (1) The garden of Eden, when all things were as God intended. (2) From the fall to the present. This realm is debilitated by Satan, sickness, social oppression, fractured community, enmity between humankind and nature, violence, death. (3) The apocalypse, when God invades the present world and interrupts history. (4) The reinstitution of the original purposes of God (the reign of God). The end time will be like the beginning time of Genesis 1.

According to the earliest Christians, the mission of God is underway through Jesus. Although the Second Testament reveals a diversity of perspectives, this literature shares the conviction that the ministry, death, and resurrection of Jesus are signs of the divine restoration. In the apocalyptic tradition, the mission of God will be complete when Jesus returns.

The writer of Ephesians catches the cosmic scope of the *missio dei*. God's plan, for the fullness of time, is "to gather up all things in him, things in heaven and things on earth" (Ephesians 1:10). The early Christian community understood itself to participate in this mission.

Between the ascension and return of Jesus, the mission of the church is to interpret the signs of the times, to call for repentance, to

---

[4]Emphasis added.

baptize, and to teach. Jewish people are not exhorted to leave Judaism and enter Christianity as a new religion, but to recognize that the God of Israel is at work through Christ to bless all nations. Gentiles are to repent. Bringing the gospel to the nations (Gentiles) is a centerpiece of Christian mission (Mark 13:10; cf. Matthew 28:19; Luke 24:47). The *missio dei* includes embodying the divine purposes in the community (e.g., Matthew 7:21–27; 24:36–25:46).

Preaching is integral to mission. Paul, for instance, says, "For the message about the cross [i.e., the preaching of the cross as revealing God's apocalyptic transformation of the world] is foolishness to those who are perishing, but to us who are being saved it is the power of God" (1 Corinthians 1:18). Preaching makes God's eschatological agency through Christ a present reality for the listeners. "Faith comes from what is heard, and what is heard comes through the word [preaching] of Christ" (Romans 10:17).

The gospels and Acts, together with Paul, stress that the church will meet resistance to its mission (e.g., Mark 13:9–12; Acts 4:1–22; John 15:18–16:4). The Spirit empowers the community to continue its witness, even in the face of opposition.

These basic approaches to mission continued from the late biblical period until Constantine.[5] The church understood itself as an outpost of the new age that was living within the old. The mission of the church was to alert people to the dangers of the old world and to invite them to prepare for the new. Preaching was a primary means for repentance, for interpreting baptism, and for teaching.

### Creating a Christian Society

With the recognition of the church by the state at the time of Constantine (313 C.E.) an important aspect of the church's perception of its mission in the West changed to include supporting the existing social order. Territories were supposed to function as Christian life systems. The church regarded the hierarchical structure of medieval society as divinely authorized. In order to be saved, one had to be a part of the church. David Bosch, a theologian of mission, speaks of "the ecclesiasticization of salvation" to describe this phenomenon.[6] Preaching played an important role.

---

[5]The story of the expansion of the church is told compactly in Stephen Neill, *A History of Christian Missions,* The Pelican History of the Church (Harmondsworth: Penguin Books, 1964); more critical analysis is found in Bosch, *Transforming Mission.*

[6]Bosch, *Transforming Mission,* 217.

At its best, this arrangement allowed the church to be the conscience of civilization and to promote love and justice throughout the social world. However, the church was easily co-opted by the state. The church sometimes approved of coercing non-Christians (e.g., Jewish people) to become Christian. A territorial approach to Christianity ensued, assuming that people living in a given land were Christian, and, therefore, were subject to the benefits and discipline of the church.

Sermons explained the nature and means of sin and salvation. They guided people in the Christian life. Preaching asserted the divine roots of the social hierarchy, the responsibilities of people at each level of the hierarchy, and the penalties for failing to do one's part in the social pyramid. Preaching was a means whereby people who were forced to become Christian could learn something of their new religion.

The Lutheran and Calvinist branches of the Reformation retain a view of the relationship of church and the social world similar to that of medievalism. These two reformers objected not to continuity of church and state, but to abuses of that relationship. At the Peace of Westphalia (1648), the territorialism of the medieval period was continued by the doctrine "Each region has to follow the religion of its ruler."[7]

For Calvinism, mission included instituting the reign of Christ in the broader social fabric.[8] Hence, in Geneva the church instructed the governors and the people in the ways of God. Preaching was a primary mode of instruction.

The Anabaptists, however, were an exception to the prevailing view of mission as creating a Christian territory.[9] Anabaptists insisted on separation between church and state. The Anabaptist churches regarded themselves as colonies of holy living who demonstrated the ways of God. In this respect, they recovered a significant emphasis in the understanding of mission that had been present in Israel and the earliest churches. Anabaptists denied that a person could be a Christian based on nothing more than living in a territory. A person could become a Christian only by conversion. The mission of the church included offering people opportunities for such transformation. Preaching participated in the Anabaptist mission by leading people to conversion and by offering guidance in life.

---

[7]Ibid., 241.
[8]Ibid., 255–60.
[9]Ibid., 245–47.

## Mission and the Enlightenment Era

The changes in the consciousness of Western civilization that occurred in connection with the Enlightenment affected the church's understanding of mission.[10] These forces include the emergence of specialized bodies of knowledge; the idea that the world is similar to a machine, with each part having its own function; the questioning of the divine right of monarchy; the belief that individuals have the right to self-determination; truth as ascertained by empirical observation or coherence with first principles; the confidence that enlightened Western culture is the height of civilization.

The development of specialized bodies of knowledge and the notion of world as machine contributed to the church's thinking of mission as an activity of the church. The church increasingly associated mission with the particular task of bringing the gospel to persons who had never received it. Christians organized mission societies, such as the Redemptorists and the London Christian Missionary Society.

These currents eroded the formal symbiotic relationship between church and state and the territorial approach to church membership. Vestiges of a territorial approach formally continue in some nations to the present day.

Many North Americans came to think that individuals should determine whether they become a part of the church. Consequently, mission began to include presenting people with the opportunity to choose whether to belong to the church.

Although the separation between church and state took place at a formal level in some countries, many people subscribed to a continuing informal alliance between church and nation. A part of the church's mission was to help mold responsible citizens so that their Christian orientation would permeate society.

Many missionaries combined the gospel message and Western culture, and presented these emphases as a single package to non-Christians. The church was a partner in colonialism, receiving new members, financial benefits, and land, while offering to local people medical, educational, and vocational opportunities.

By the late eighteenth and early nineteenth centuries, the social gospel movement sought to institute the implications of divine love and justice in the wider social world. This movement believed that Christian salvation embraced both the salvation of individuals and

---

[10]For a summary of Enlightenment ideas as they pertain to mission, see ibid., 262–74.

of society. Indeed, one of Christ's purposes (according to the social gospellers) was to create a new society on earth that functioned according to God's principles. Under the power of the Spirit, the mission of the church included working in the social world beyond the church to put these principles into practice. The social gospel movement particularly sought to end the ravages of urban poverty and exploitation.

In overseas missions, the sermon was a primary instrument through which the preacher called attention to the sinful state of non-Christian peoples, the gospel as the remedy, and the offer of repentance, baptism, and growth in faith. In the churches sending missionaries, the sermon helped the community understand the need for such mission.

## Contemporary Patterns

The modern synthesis is disintegrating and is being replaced by postmodernism marked by relativism and pluralism. In today's milieu, Christians differ regarding the ways in which North American churches should relate to the culture and to other communities: church as colony of resident aliens, or church as public community. I discuss these movements separately and then suggest that, with respect to mission, there are elements within each that complement the other.

The notion that the church is a colony of resident aliens derives from the postliberal theological movement.[11] The church is to interpret itself and the world from the perspective of the biblical narrative and other historic Christian doctrines. The church is not to adapt its message to modern standards of truth that derive from outside the Christian corpus (e.g., Enlightenment, empirical verification). Such adaptation makes the outside standard of truth the highest authority in the church.[12] The mission of the church is to be the church, a community whose life system models the ways of God.

The church is in the world as a colony of resident aliens. Aliens live in a particular community, but they are not fully integrated into the community. The mission of the church is not to transform society by engaging society on society's terms. The church articulates its distinctive vision of the world as an alternative to regnant social visions. As a form of proclamatory action, the congregation can work with other organizations to protest war, to correct systemic injustice, to feed the hungry, to house the homeless, and so on.[13]

---

[11]Stanley Hauerwas and William Willimon, *Resident Aliens* (Nashville: Abingdon Press, 1989).

[12]Ibid., 24.

[13]Ibid., 47.

The sermon seeks to help the community understand how Christians interpret the Christian faith, as well as how Christians interpret the world.[14] Preaching teaches the congregation the language of faith. The sermon leads the Christian community to grasp its purpose as a colony modeling God's ways.

The great virtue of this approach to the church is that it does not trade distinctive Christian identity for contemporary trinkets.[15] However, some postliberals seem to regard the culture as altogether opposed to the gospel. Occasionally postliberals give the impression that the Christian community has nothing to learn from the world. One sometimes gets the inkling that the model social world is one in which all other persons and communities join the church. When speaking of *the* Christian story, postliberals sometimes fail to acknowledge pluralism within the Christian community itself.[16]

The designation "public church" is often associated with revisionary theology, but it can embrace aspects of other movements (e.g., liberation theology).[17] This church is public in two senses: (a) It understands itself as a member of the wider community. It engages other communities. It participates fully in the social world, affecting and being affected by that world. (b) Its standards of truth are open to public scrutiny.

The mission of this church is to engage in mutual critical correlation between Christian tradition and the culture. The engagement is mutual by going from tradition to culture and from culture to tradition. It is also critical; the tradition criticizes the culture, and the culture criticizes the tradition. It is correlational by assuming that adequate understandings of God and the world emerge from conversation between tradition and culture. Hence, the public church criticizes contemporary culture from the perspective of the culture and seeks to affect that culture accordingly. It also criticizes its understanding of Christian tradition from the perspective of contemporary insights.

A great strength of this movement is that it seeks to combine faithfulness to the core of Christian tradition with contemporaneity.

---

[14]Ronald Allen, *Interpreting the Gospel: An Introduction to Preaching* (St. Louis: Chalice Press, 1998), 76. Cf. Charles M. Campbell, *Preaching Jesus: New Directions for Homiletics in Hans Frei's Postliberal Theology* (Grand Rapids: Wm. B. Eerdmans, 1997), and the contributions by Scott Black Johnston in Ronald J. Allen, Barbara Shires Blaisdell, and Scott Black Johnston, *Theology for Preaching: Authority, Truth and Knowledge of God in a Postmodern Ethos* (Nashville: Abingdon Press, 1997).

[15]Ibid., 77.

[16]Cf. Ronald Allen, in Allen, Blaisdell, and Johnston, *Theology for Preaching*, 143–44.

[17]Ibid., 144–45.

People can truly believe this church's promises because they are confirmed by publicly verifiable standards. It can work with other people and groups to help manifest values of love and justice in the social world. Critics object that the contemporary world often plays an overbearing role in determining what is credible.

I have sharply drawn the lines of these two movements to emphasize their distinctiveness. However, the two visions are not so much diametric opposites as they are differences of emphasis. The postliberal emphasis on developing distinctive Christian identity helps the whole church remember that Christian identity does not come naturally. In order to witness effectively and with integrity, the church must learn who it is and what it is to be about. A major purpose of nurturing Christian identity is so that the church can engage in mission. I know of no public church theologians who would disagree with this claim. Furthermore, leading postliberals intensely engage in social witness.[18] At the same time, the revisionary emphasis on the public witness of the church reminds us that the church exists not for itself but for the world. While the Fourth Gospel loads its vocabulary in special ways, it does no violence to Johannine thought to recollect that God loves the *world* and seeks to redeem it (John 3:16). I know of no postliberal theologians who would disagree with this claim.

## A Theology of Mission

A good theology of mission begins with the character of God. Christians affirm with Charles Wesley that God, confirmed through Christ, is "pure, unbounded love."[19] God relates to the world with unconditional love and seeks for all inhabitants of the world to live in love. In this vein, I speak of the gospel as the promise of God's unconditional love for each and all and God's will for justice for each and all.

The recognition that God is unreserved love combines with another key insight: God is omnipresent. God is ever at work throughout the world to help the world become a cosmic community of love and justice. The *missio dei* is for the world to become the community of abundance and mutual support that is pictured in the opening chapter of Genesis and in other key moments of the Bible and Christian tradition.

---

[18]See Stanley P. Saunders and Charles L. Campbell, *The Word on the Street: Performing the Scriptures in the Urban Context* (Grand Rapids: Wm. B. Eerdmans, 2000).

[19]Charles Wesley, "Love Divine, All Loves Excelling," in *Chalice Hymnal* (St. Louis: Chalice Press, 1995), 517. I borrow this expression from its frequent use by Schubert Ogden, e.g., *The Reality of God* (New York: Harper and Row, 1963), 177.

Since God is at work in all times and places, communities other than the church (and persons other than Christians) participate in the mission of God. God works through persons and communities who are unaware that they are joining in the divine mission. Consequently, the church can enter into partnership, as a part of the Christian practice of hospitality, with other entities to work toward love and justice.

The divine omnipresence does not mean that God approves of everything that the church does, nor that God approves of everything that takes place in the world. God grieves over idolatry, injustice, oppression, alienation, and pain. (The church itself can manifest these qualities!) God calls communities to acknowledge the contrast between the divine purposes and their behavior, to repent, and to conform to God's purposes.[20]

The church does not need to create a mission program. The church is to join God in the mission in which God is already engaged. For example, in the next part of the chapter, I speak specifically of evangelism and social witness. However, though such specific activities may express the mission of the church, they are not the sum total of that mission. They are expressions or modes of the more comprehensive mission.

The church is to interpret the implications of the *missio dei* for the sake of the world. The church's first concern is not to build up its institutional life, but to point to God's intentions in the wider world, to join God in those aims, and to help others recognize and respond.

Because a congregation is finite, it cannot engage in the whole of God's mission at one time. Furthermore, congregations live in specific contexts. Consequently, a congregation should identify the aspects of the *missio dei* that are most important to its context. To help particularize the implications of the gospel, many congregations now articulate mission statements, as described in the previous chapter, that help a local Christian community understand its *particular* witness to the gospel in its neighborhood, region, and denomination.

---

[20]I am keenly aware that some passages in the Bible and in subsequent Christian thought assert that God actively brings painful judgment on individuals and communities who do not embody the divine purposes. However, as indicated elsewhere, I do not believe that God can maintain integrity and act thus. I understand the deeper intention of that way of speaking to mean that persons and communities often suffer the consequences of their own violations of God's purposes, and from the wider brokenness of the world. See further Clark M. Williamson and Ronald J. Allen, *A Credible and Timely Word: Process Theology and Preaching* (St. Louis: Chalice Press, 1992), 107–10.

In so doing, the church engages in the Christian practices of struggling to interpret the congregation's interlocking contexts to identify the witnesses most needed (especially naming the principalities and powers) and of listening attentively to one another to identify those acts of service and witness that the congregation is most able to undertake. Mission includes maintaining social structures that sustain life as God intends.

## Evangelism as an Expression of Mission

The word "evangelism" is from the Greek word *euaggelion,* usually translated "good news" or "gospel." From this general point of view, evangelism can be understood as all that takes place in the congregation that witnesses to God's unconditional love for each and all and God's irrepressible summons to justice for each and all.[21] The handling of an infant in the nursery, the lesson in Bible school, decisions made by the board, the support group for deserted women, marching on city hall, expressing solidarity with persons in a situation of repression in another nation—in the broad sense, all such aspects of Christian life are evangelism.[22] However, in many congregations today, evangelism usually refers to offering a Christian interpretation of the meaning of life to persons who do not embrace such an interpretation. Although some readers will find this definition too narrow, it provides a useful focus for the following overview of an important and contested aspect of the *missio dei.*[23]

Evangelism as making a Christian interpretation of life available to non-Christians is important for the church's relationship with persons who have minimal vision of transcendent reality and who measure the meaning of life on the basis of finite values (i.e., idolatry). I think particularly of persons who have no formal religious affiliation, though persons within religious communities can fall into this category.

Of course, God is ever at work for the good of all (even idolaters). However, the church is to make the gospel available to people who

---

[21]For critique of the notion of evangelism as all that the church does, see Mortimer Arias, "That the World May Believe," *International Review of Mission* 65 (1976): 13–26.

[22]For survey, see Pope-Levison, 231–43.

[23]Evangelism is sometimes equated with "church growth." The two notions are neither mutually exclusive nor synonymous. I take "church growth" to refer to a broad range of activities designed to bring about an increase in congregational membership. Church growth activities can be addressed to persons who are already Christian but who are seeking a new congregational home. Evangelism, as I use it, refers to offering the gospel to persons who have not embraced it. Although evangelism should bring people into Christian community, the basic goal of evangelism is not an increase in church membership per se but helping people discover and respond to the gospel.

do not have a transcendent perspective on life; when people recognize God's presence and purposes, God has more elbow room to communicate unconditional love and the divine will for justice than when people do not acknowledge transcendent presence and purposes. When people recognize the God of Israel as the universal source of love and the power of justice, they are better able to identify lesser gods and goods, and, thereby, to be saved from much of the damage that is done by idolatry, false trust, and injustice. Furthermore, God rejoices when people trust the gospel and live in its way.

Preaching can help with this aspect of evangelism, but as I note below, relatively few people who are not interested in the gospel come to conventional services of worship.

Thinking of the church as a life system intersects directly with the mission of the church in this regard. Some congregations in long-established denominations in North America have programs for membership recruitment (e.g., taking pies to persons who visit the Sunday service). But, despite the fact that strategies for helping non-Christians encounter Christian vision are available, relatively few congregations employ them.[24] Aside from efforts by the Roman Catholic and Episcopal churches to recover the ancient catechumenate (instruction for initiating adults into the church), typical congregations in the long-established denominations have few ministries to help persons who are curious about Christianity get basic information about Christian faith.[25]

For the church to fulfill this aspect of mission, a major agenda item for the future is to mobilize the church to make the gospel available to persons who have little vision of transcendent reality. Congregations need to articulate the gospel evangelistically outside their walls. Churches need to find ways that the sermon can perform one of its oldest evangelistic tasks—inviting people to the decision of whether to accept the love of God through Christ as the basis for their self-understanding.

Evangelism as making a Christian interpretation of life available to non-Christians intersects with the church's relationship with members of other religions. The church does not need to convert all

---

[24]See George C. Hunter III, *How to Reach Secular People* (Nashville: Abingdon Press, 1992), esp. 55–72.

[25]The Roman Catholic Church and the Episcopal Church have developed catechumenates to introduce people to Christian vision, e.g., *RCIA: Rite of Christian Initiation of Adults,* Study Edition (Collegeville: The Liturgical Press, 1988), and *The Cutting Edge of Mission: A Report of the Mid-Point Review of the Decade of Evangelism,* ed. Cyril C. Okorocha (London: Anglican Communion Publications, 1996).

persons of other religions. Jewish people, for instance, already serve the living God. God is at work in other religions to mediate divine love and a call for just living.

Some Christians assert that all religions have the same essence. Other Christians believe that persons can live full and authentic lives by following religious paths other than Christianity. To be frank, I do not know enough about other religions to gauge the accuracy of these claims. However, it follows from the divine omnipresence that God works through all religions (even if all religions do not have the same essence or even if people do not reach the deepest possibilities for living through other religions). The relativity of human perception means that Christianity can learn from other religions, and that other religions can learn from Christianity. However, this process involves careful exploration.

The church can often work in partnership with adherents of other religions to seek a more just world. For instance, my colleague Clark M. Williamson notes that Christians do not have a mission *to* Judaism (i.e., conversion) but a mission *with* Judaism to witness to the one God and to work jointly to end anti-Semitism and other injustices.[26]

This direction does not mean that the church has no evangelistic mission with respect to persons of other religions. Marjorie Suchocki, former Dean of Claremont School of Theology, explains,

> Human beings are a peculiar lot, and while groups of us do very well sharing characteristics and sensitivities that mark us as being...Americans, or participants in a certain cultural matrix, there are always those who cannot fit the dominant mode. Not all of those in a western culture find Christianity a route to their own well being; not all those in an Asian country will experience well being through Buddhism. Missionary experience, whether Christian or Buddhist, has shown that there are always a few in a culture who are not met by the religions of their own environment. Because these are few, should we feel no concern?[27]

This task is important for mission both in other lands and in North America. North Americans now encounter Muslims, Buddhists, Hindus, native African religionists, and others in the neighborhood, at school, and at work.

---

[26]Clark M. Williamson, *A Mutual Witness: Toward Critical Solidarity between Jews and Christians* (St. Louis: Chalice Press, 1992).

[27]Marjorie Suchocki, *God, Christ, Church: A Practical Guide to Process Theology,* rev. ed. (New York: Crossroad, 1989), 159.

To be sure, aspects of other religions can be inadequate. For instance, a subgroup in another religion may glorify killing human beings. Consequently, the evangelistic mission among other religions includes the delicate task of challenging aspects of those religions that subvert the divine purposes. However, Christians need to undertake such analysis with humility. Our own tradition has sometimes manifested the errors that we find in others.

## Witness for a Just World

The quest for a just world is an aspect of mission for which many ministers in the long-established denominations have deep passion. By "just world" I mean a world with the relationships shown in Genesis 1. Preaching can play an important role in this mode of mission.

Many injustices (e.g., racism and sexism) are systemic. They are not simply the result of personal attitudes and actions, but are functions of systems in the larger culture. Of course, individuals also manifest such distortions of God's aims for the cosmic family. For instance, as I write, a European American racist just killed an African American and a Korean, and wounded several Jewish persons. But racism is deeper than warped individuals. Racism is entrenched prejudice on the part of European Americans combined with the power to exploit persons of color.

Racism is so entrenched in the United States that a workshop on racism, held at Christian Theological Seminary, demonstrated that it is impossible for European Americans not to be racist. European Americans inherently benefit from the racist system even when we are against racism. Until systemic change occurs, the highest hope for a European American is to be an antiracist racist.

Formal, informal, and tacit factors are significant. The historic denominations have made formal statements against racism and other forms of repression. However, racism functions informally in many congregations. For instance, very few European American congregations call African Americans as pastors.

At one level, the church seeks to confront such systems with the gospel. However, systems are resistant. People who benefit from systemic evil are slow to repent. Systemic change is slow. Preachers need to help congregations endure protracted confrontation with agents of brokenness.

At another level, the mission of the church includes hands-on healing ministries. For instance, one of our daughters has just returned from a mission trip to New Mexico on which she joined Native Americans in the struggle for economic liberation by building corrals to improve cattle raising. Many Christians work regularly in shelters for the abused, clothing stores, foster care, and collecting supplies to send to areas ravaged by natural disaster.

Such acts of witness provide material help for persons in distress. They represent God's will for justice for all. Many Christians feel overwhelmed, powerless, and paralyzed in the face of mammoth systemic challenges. Such persons feel empowered by helping other people. Yet individual actions seldom change systemic forces. The congregation needs to be involved in systemic change.

Injustice ravages the internal life of the church as well as the external world. Racism, gender prejudice, homophobia, and other defilements of the divine purpose take place inside the church. The preacher needs to address them.

Evangelism and witness for justice are specific expressions of mission. Opening the lens wider, we recognize that mission is all that happens in the life of the congregation, for all that happens in the congregation (both internally and in the congregation's relationship with the larger world) can participate in the *missio dei.* The theology of mission recommended in this chapter pushes us to recognize that mission is all that Christians do. Every arena of life can be a mission field, and this mission can be encouraged weekly through preaching.

The home is a mission field. The resident(s)—whether a single person and animals, a family, or persons who have formed a voluntary community—can practice love and justice in relationships with one another, with the neighborhood, and with the wider world. Engaging in daily worship in the home, dealing with each other so as to reflect gospel values, having a lifestyle that makes modest demands on the environment, helping neighbors be responsible for one another, recycling, making socially responsible financial investments, confronting household members with violations of covenantal community, empathizing with household members, participating in activities that protest injustice—these are examples of ways in which the household can manifest the *missio dei.*

Similar mission fields include school, workplace, civic arena, and social relationships. Christians have opportunities to relate to others from the perspective of knowing that God loves all persons unconditionally and that God wills justice for all. An elementary school teacher is not simply performing a job, but is embodying the mission of the church in the way in which she relates to the students and the school.

I used to say that the mission field begins at the edge of the church parking lot. I was wrong. The mission field begins at the edge of the human heart and includes the congregation itself.

## Preaching as Mission[28]

Most Christian preaching takes place in worship. In the broad sense, the Christian practice of worship is a missionary activity in that it liturgically dramatizes God's gracious relationship with the world and the human response. This liturgical enactment sets forth a vision of God for both congregation and wider world. Elements of worship can take on a missionary quality. For instance, mission sometimes calls for financial resources for disaster relief in another part of the country. Receiving the offering is participation in the *missio dei.*

The sermon can tell the Christian story in such a way as to help the congregation interpret the mission of the local church as part of God's mission. The sermon names the significance of the unconditional love of God for the congregation and its setting as well as God's will for justice.[29] The preacher seeks to help the community identify how it can participate in the divine mission.

The sermon should be a part of a conversation in the congregation concerning the relationship of the church with the relativism and pluralism of postmodernity. This conversation relies on the Christian practice of attentive listening—not only to other Christians but also to those outside the church. Given the relativity of human perception, Christians can easily lose confidence in the trustworthiness of the gospel. As a student said plaintively, "*Why* should I believe that I can count on God any more than I believe that I can count on a character from a science fiction movie?" The mission of the preacher includes helping the congregation learn why we can rely on the gospel.

Furthermore, if God is active at all times and in all places for the good of the world, why should Christians commit themselves to the church, especially when the church is often a step behind the divine purposes? Preaching can help people understand why it can be important to be a part of Christian community. Christian practices of

---

[28]*Journal for Preachers* often features articles that relate preaching and mission. See the following articles, for example, which focus intensively on preaching and mission: Darrell L. Guder, "Missional Theology for a Missional Church," vol. 22, no. 1 (1999): 3–11; Douglas John Hall, "Stewardship as a Missional Discipline," vol. 22, no. 1 (1999): 19–28; Iain Russell-Jones, "In the Heart of the Conflict: Jacques Ellul and Christian Mission," vol. 22, no. 2 (2000): 3–8; Catherine Gunsalus Gonzalez, "Mission Accomplished, Mission Begun: Lent and the Book of Revelation," vol. 22, no. 2 (2000): 9–13; Donald W. Shriver, Jr., "Missionary Repertoire," vol. 22, no 2 (2000): 14–20; William H. Willimon, "Preaching as Missionary Encounter with North American Paganism," vol. 22, no. 3 (2000): 3–10; Carlos F. Cordoza-Orlandi, "What Makes Preaching 'Missional?'" vol. 22, no. 4 (2000): 3–9; Cheryl Bridges Johns, "When All God's People Are Prophets: Acts and the Task of Missional Preaching," vol. 22, no. 4 (2000): 16–21.

[29]Cf. Allen, *Interpreting the Gospel,* and Mary Catherine Hilkert, *Naming Grace: Preaching and the Sacramental Imagination* (New York: Continuum, 1997).

tolerating one another in failures and encouraging one another to conform more fully to the gospel are often key to maintaining the congregation as a vital community.

In addition, the sermon *is* mission. At its best, the sermon, empowered by the Holy Spirit, can effect the realities it speaks. For instance, the sermon that announces God's love for all evokes the awareness of being loved in the congregation.

By definition God is present and active in each stage of the sermon: from the moment of awareness that the preacher must prepare a sermon, through the conception of the sermon, through its preparation and embodiment (delivery), to the effects of the sermon in the congregation. God is the quintessential participant in the life system of the congregation, for God is simultaneously present with all members of the community. God tries to help the preacher articulate an adequate vision. God seeks to help the congregation be receptive to the message and to act on the sermon.

God is present throughout the process of preparation and preaching through thoughts, intuitions, and feelings that come to the preacher. However, every idea and impulse that drifts into the window of the preacher's consciousness is not borne on the wings of the Holy Spirit. The preacher is susceptible to ideas that minimize divine intentions. In order to gauge whether a thought, intuition, or feeling is leading in a direction that can serve the gospel, the preacher can analyze that idea by the criteria of appropriateness to the gospel, intelligibility, and moral plausibility.

Preacher and congregation can say yes to such impulses, or they can turn away. When they respond affirmatively, the opportunities for the sermon to cooperate with God's purposes are increased. When the pastor and the community respond negatively, such opportunities diminish. In the case of a negative choice, God works with the community to help come to expression through the sermon as much of the divine vision of love and justice as possible, and to minimize potentially limiting effects.

## In-Church Preaching and Out-Church Preaching

David G. Buttrick, a leading professor of preaching at Vanderbilt University, makes a suggestive distinction for thinking about preaching and mission: in-church preaching and out-church preaching.[30] Most preaching takes place inside the church. From the standpoint of mission, in-church preaching nurtures the congregation in the gospel

[30]David G. Buttrick, *Homiletic: Moves and Structures* (Philadelphia: Fortress Press, 1987), 225–29.

and helps the congregation act on the mission of the church. Most clergy are prepared through seminary training and weekly practice for in-church preaching.

Out-church preaching takes place outside the established congregation. According to Buttrick, out-church preaching is the responsibility of lay members. Although such preaching occasionally takes place in formal settings (e.g., lay-sponsored meetings in prison), it typically takes place informally as laity encounter people in day-to-day settings.

I applaud Buttrick as one of a handful of authors to consider preaching outside the church. However, Professor Buttrick's proposal for out-church preaching needs a supplement. Few laity are currently able to give an account of Christian hope. Lay Christians need to be sensitized to their call to this ministry and trained for it.[31] As the long-standing denominations shrink in membership, the evangelistic potential of Christians personally interacting with non-Christians shrinks. The church needs additional strategies for attempting to spark the consciousness of contemporary people toward the gospel.

We are in an experimental time in these matters. For example, recognizing that Christian faith involves direct involvement in human community, many congregations in the historic denominations have eschewed a presence in the electronic media because they do not want people to substitute television for living community. Such congregations overlook opportunities for experimenting with other modes of Christian presence in the media. For instance, a one-minute radio spot lingers with me. A preschool child tries to get on a parent's calendar so they can spend time together. The parent is too busy. The child's voice ends with a provocative invitation to consider the ways in which we use our time. The spot ends simply "This message is brought to you by such-and-such Church, which worships at 9:30 a.m. at such-and-such address." That message comes to mind every time one of our children asks me to do something and I reply, "Not now." Each time I pass that church building, I wonder, "Could they help me get my life priorities in order?" This spot is an experiment in evangelism that works in my case.

---

[31]For an approach to preparing laity to preach, see Douglas Gwyn, "A School of the Prophets: Teaching Congregational Members to Preach," in *Preaching in the Context of Worship,* ed. David M. Greenhaw and Ronald J. Allen (St. Louis: Chalice Press, 2000), 99–108.

With the dawn of the new millennium, many people are searching for the deeper purposes of life. The success of many "seeker services" is consistent with this observation.[32] The time is ripe for ministers to add out-church preaching to their preaching portfolios. At present, preachers in the historic churches have few contemporary models for such preaching.[33] Hence, preachers need to experiment with evangelistic sermons. For instance, a preacher might begin by asking basic questions: What questions are people asking today? What issues haunt or captivate us? Can the preacher segue from these kinds of questions and issues to the gospel, or vice versa? How can the preacher talk about the gospel so as to show its promise for the listeners while honoring its integrity? What evidences of the truth of the gospel will today's listeners find compelling?

Preachers may also need to experiment with modes and occasions for evangelistic preaching. The seeker service is such a venue. Is it possible to preach in the electronic media without creating an electronic church? I can imagine an evangelistic sermon taking place in a rented auditorium, theater, or conference room over lunch. I wonder if preachers from the long-established denominations could reclaim a version of open-air preaching by articulating the gospel in parks or malls or other places where people gather.

The preacher can help the congregation clarify the relationship between Christian faith and other faiths. For instance, an acquaintance confesses, "I feel that I am supposed to try to convert my Muslim neighbor, but then I don't feel that I should." Good preaching can help resolve this confusion by clarifying the relationship between Christianity and Islam.

## Preaching as Witness for Justice

Preaching is an important component of the church's mission for justice. Sin seduces many people to think that brokenness is normal.

---

[32]From my perspective, the seeker service is not a fully developed service of worship, but an occasion when the gospel is introduced to persons who are seeking meaning in life.

[33]See William H. Willimon, *The Intrusive Word: Preaching to the Unbaptized* (Grand Rapids: William. B. Eerdmans, 1994); William H. Willimon and Stanley Hauerwas, *Preaching to Strangers: Evangelism in Today's World* (Louisville: Westminster/John Knox Press, 1992); and Craig Loscalzo, *Evangelistic Preaching that Connects: Guidance in Shaping Fresh and Appealing Sermons* (Downers Grove, Ill.: InterVarsity Press, 1995).

A basic calling of the preacher is to alert the congregation to the fact that injustice contradicts the divine will.[34] The preacher can also help the congregation understand such situations in detail.[35] What factors bring about such systemic phenomena? How do such circumstances deny God's promise of love and call for justice? The preacher can help the congregation envision alternatives to the present. The sermon can help the congregation form an image of how the world can be different, so that the congregation can live toward that vision. The sermon can identify steps that the congregation can take.

Many congregations today have an insular view of mission, as if they need only serve their own members or neighborhoods. The preacher can help such a congregation understand that it is part of a global community in which all persons and communities are connected. As Clark M. Williamson, a Disciples theologian, says, "We, God, and everybody and everything else are caught up in a big Koinonial web."[36]

The sermon can help the congregation understand that mission today should not be a one-way street between helper and helpee, but should take the form of partnership, thereby embodying the recognition of the gospel that all people (and nature) are interrelated. The sermon can help the community identify fruitful partnerships.

An irony: While many pastors in the long-established denominations have a passionate commitment to justice, they preach very few sermons that explore an issue of injustice in detail.[37] Preachers

---

[34]Cf. Walter Burghardt, *Preaching the Just Word* (Yale: Yale University Press, 1998); David G. Buttrick, *Preaching the New and the Now* (Louisville: Westminster/John Knox Press, 1998); id., *A Captive Voice;* James H. Harris, *Preaching Liberation,* Fortress Resources for Preaching (Minneapolis: Fortress Press, 1995); Justo L. Gonzalez and Catherine G. Gonzalez, *The Liberating Pulpit* (Nashville: Abingdon Press, 1994); Christine M. Smith *Preaching as Weeping, Confession, and Resistance: Radical Responses to Radical Evil.* (Louisville: Westminster/John Knox Press, 1992); William K. McElvaney, *Preaching from Camelot to Covenant: Announcing God's Action in the World* (Nashville: Abingdon Press, 1989); William J. Nottingham, *The Practice and Preaching of Liberation* (St. Louis: CBP Press, 1988); for preaching on controversial issues, see Ronald J. Allen, *Preaching the Topical Sermon* (Louisville: Westminster/John Knox Press, 1992), 95–112.

[35]For understandings of justice from the perspectives of persons with disabilities, Native Americans, African Americans, Filipino Americans, Hispanic Americans, Korean Americans, Jewish people, gay and lesbian people, see *Preaching Justice: Ethnic and Cultural Perspectives,* ed. Christine Marie Smith (Cleveland: The Pilgrim Press, 1999).

[36]Clark M. Williamson, "Good Stewards of God's Varied Grace," *Encounter* 47 (1986): 77.

[37]Ronald J. Allen, "What Are We Really Preaching?" *Pulpit Digest* 78/5 (1997), 78–85; cf. Buttrick, *A Captive Voice,* 9–10.

tend to mention such issues only in passing (a technique I call "sideswiping"). Issues of injustice are not often considered elsewhere in the congregation. Consequently, the community often has a low awareness of the theological importance of such issues, as well as little direct motivation for engaging in mission to address them, and little guidance in how to do so.

The degree to which a congregation is receptive to a sermon on a social issue, especially on a controversial topic, is often directly related to the relationship of the minister with the congregation's life system. When a congregation and a pastor live in a relationship of trust, a congregation tends to be willing to entertain ideas that challenge and enlarge their present ways of thinking and acting. When the relationship is dysfunctional, the congregation is seldom willing to consider alternative modes of relating to the issue, regardless of how brilliant the preacher's theological analysis or how evocative the preacher's language and embodiment.

Telling stories of particular individuals and communities helps the sermon put human faces on issues of injustice. For instance, telling a story of a particular African American who suffers from racism is one of the most effective ways to help a European American congregation understand the importance of the issue.

I sometimes hear people in the church complain because they are tired of the church trying to be p.c. (politically correct) on matters of justice. One of the preacher's most important services, in today's polarized climate, is to help the congregation understand that the church is not seeking to be p.c., but t.c. (theologically correct).

## Life Is Mission

Sermons can help sensitize the congregation to this comprehensive understanding of mission. The preacher seeks to help the members of the congregation ask of every situation in life, How can I best manifest God's love for all and God's will for justice for all? At first, people may need consciously to will this question into self-awareness. However, the notion of Christian practice leads us to realize that analyzing situations from this perspective can become almost intuitive.

The preacher does not simply plead for members to live individually as Christians. Christian identity is communal. Christians, even when alone, represent the Christian community. The preacher aims to help Christians recognize that in every one of their everyday affairs, they have an opportunity to embody Christian faith.

Of course, the preacher must sometimes call the community to recognize that they are not living the Christian mission in the home or beyond. The sermon can help people recognize necessary acts of repentance, reconciliation, and restoration.

## Implications for Preachers

The life of the congregation *is* mission. The mission of the church is to participate in the *missio dei,* the mission of God to transform the world into a community of love, justice, and abundance for all creatures. Everything that happens in the congregation is to embody the divine realm so that the very life of the community represents that realm. Particular actions express the divine realm. For instance, the church as mission comes to expression through evangelism and through witness for justice. The sermon is more than talking about mission. Preaching is itself mission. The sermon can contribute to the missionary life of the congregation through several venues:

- Help the church name the *missio dei* as the sum total of the purposes of God for the sake of the entire world and a mission in which the church is called and empowered to participate.

- Help the church discover or remember that mission is not a function within the congregation's life but is its fundamental identity. The congregational system is supposed to bring the reign of God to expression.

- Help the community recognize the shift in emphasis that has taken place from thinking of mission as something that the church does (particularly in far-away places) to the realization that mission encompasses all that the church is and does.

- Model mission by telling mission stories from the pulpit.

- Help the congregation reflect on the degree to which the community's life participates adequately in the *missio dei.* To what degree does the congregation truly represent the reign of God? At what points does the congregational system need to be reformed in order to better represent the mission of God?

- Find fresh avenues for evangelistic witness, especially through preaching, among persons who have minimal vision of the transcendent.

- Help the congregation envision ways of relating to other religions, and persons who follow them, in ways that are appropriate to the gospel, intelligible, and morally credible.

- Help the congregation recognize injustice.

- Help the congregation identify systemic and personal forms of injustice and means whereby the Christian community can call for their reform.

- Prepare the congregation for the fact that injustice is deeply entrenched and is profoundly resistant to repentance. The preacher needs to help prepare the community for a long and wrenching struggle with injustice.

- Help the congregation name injustice within its own life, and point the way toward repentance and renewal.

- Help the congregation recognize why we resist helping others or enacting other expressions of Christian mission.

- Help the congregation recognize how Christian practices come into play in the administrative life of the congregation, such as tolerating one another in failure.

- Encourage the congregation to think of all congregational activities, including ones that seem to be mainly for institutional maintenance, from the perspective of mission.

- Invite members of the congregation to generate creative ideas for expressing the mission of the church through particular actions.

- Help the congregation envision how it might better organize its membership and committees to participate more fully in the *missio dei*.

## Implications for Theories of Mission

Leaders in thinking about mission can help preachers come to a deeper grasp of the claim that preaching is itself mission. When it first hits the ear, the idea that preaching *is* mission is highly energizing. But I find it difficult to specify the meaning and significance of that claim. Of course, the sermon names the *missio dei* and invites the congregation to participate in that mission. But in what further ways is the sermon *mission?* For instance, contemporary philosophy of language emphasizes the power of language to bring into being the realities of which it speaks. In what ways can the sermon help speak into existence the cosmic community of love, justice, and abundance that God purposes?[38]

---

[38]E.g., David Schnasa Jacobsen, *Preaching in the New Creation: The Promise of New Testament Apocalyptic Texts* (Louisville: Westminster John Knox Press, 1999) and Larry Paul Jones and Jerry L. Sumney, *Preaching Apocalyptic Texts,* Preaching Classic Texts Series (St. Louis: Chalice Press, 1999).

Members of the congregation (and preachers, too) sometimes feel overwhelmed by the prospect of engaging in the *missio dei*. The world as it is today is such a great distance from being the community of love, justice, and abundance that God intends. Our resources seem so small in comparison to the need. We easily feel overwhelmed, and our efforts seem insignificant. Missiology could help congregants and preachers by identifying practical and manageable ways that members of local congregations can live out the mission of God in their everyday worlds.

Preachers can encourage missionaries in traditional forms of mission to chronicle activities in their mission fields that preachers can use as stories from the pulpit. Such stories not only add interest and credibility to the sermon but also help the congregation envision how to engage in specific expressions of mission.

Preachers who follow the Christian year and the lectionary need resources to help them understand the major doctrinal themes of the Christian year and the passages in the lectionary from the perspective of the *missio dei*. Many resources to help pastors preach from the Christian year and the lectionary are ecclesiocentric. Such materials have the virtue of building up the congregation in the gospel, but they do not always urge the congregation to participate in the larger purposes of God in the world.

## Suggestions for Further Reading

Abraham, William J. *The Logic of Evangelism* (Grand Rapids: Wm. B. Eerdmans, 1989). Considers evangelism from a theological point of view.

Guder, Darrell L., ed., *Missional Church: A Vision for the Sending of the Church in North America* (Grand Rapids: Wm. B. Eerdmans, 1998). Description of the church as a community whose identity *is* mission.

Knitter, Paul. *No Other Name: A Critical Survey of Christian Attitudes Towards the World Religions* (Maryknoll: Orbis Books, 1985). Reviews and critiques various ways Christians view and relate to other religions.

Newbigin, Lesslie. *The Open Secret: An Introduction to the Theology of Mission* (Grand Rapids: William B. Eerdmans, 1995). Influential statement of the mission of the church as participation in the *missio dei*.

# 6

# THE PREACHER AS
# SPIRITUAL LEADER

Helping the congregation live faithfully as a spiritual community is at the heart of the preacher's calling. Although the term *spiritual* is as old as the Bible, it requires careful definition, for this term and its cognates are used in many ways in the contemporary church. Furthermore, the church and the world contain multiple forms of spirituality. Each type of spirituality has distinct practices.

I use the term *spirituality* to speak of ways in which human beings attempt to become attuned to the presence and purposes of God and to live in the light of that presence. Spirituality involves Christian practices through which we become aware of the divine. Spirituality eventuates in patterns of thinking, feeling, and acting. Because spiritual awareness is interpretive, spirituality includes methods and criteria for reflecting on the adequacy of its sources and the conclusions that we draw from them.

In this chapter I first offer a typology of three basic approaches to spirituality. The heart of the chapter explores ways in which preaching flows from spirituality and nurtures spirituality. The chapter concludes by stressing the importance of the preacher's maintaining a vital spiritual life. Throughout, I note the role of Christian practice in forming and maintaining this spirituality.

Christian spirituality is personal. We individually need to claim and practice it. However, it is not private, that is, affecting us only as individuals. Because Christian faith inevitably brings us into relationship with others, Christian spirituality is personal-in-community. It strengthens us as persons so that we can be responsible members of the witnessing community. The community helps strengthen us spiritually.

## Three Types of Spirituality

I offer a simple typology of three basic approaches to Christian spirituality. Each approach contains many varieties. Each approach has its own nuances. Although I discuss the three approaches as discrete categories, a community may predominately follow one form of piety while integrating elements of others into it.

### *The Inner Life*

The "inner life" approach to spirituality assumes that God is present in the inner life—in intuition, images, and thoughts that come in contemplation. Persons who follow this path listen attentively for the movement of God in their personal experience. Contemplatives sometimes follow a set of spiritual exercises that help them shed the impediments of the ordinary world and focus on the voice of God in the self.

Contemplation typically follows one of two paths. Kataphatic contemplation (from the Greek *kataphatikos*, "affirmative") is the path of affirmation. The kataphatic contemplative seeks to make as many positive statements (affirmations) about God as possible, usually by analogy from the highest good we observe in the world. For instance, the positive experiences of the mother-child relationship reveal something of God. The kataphatic tradition does not describe the fullness of God but offers analogies that stir us with deep awareness of God. The *Spiritual Exercises* of Ignatius are influential expressions of kataphatic contemplation. These exercises lead the believer to imaginatively enter the life, death, and resurrection of Christ. Spiritual reality thereby becomes known to the community.[1]

Apophatic contemplation (from the Greek *apophatikos*, "negative") is the path of negation. The goal of apophatic contemplation is to remove as many barriers as possible between the self and God. Eventually the apophatic enters a realm of perception that is not

---

[1]Ignatius, *The Spiritual Exercises of St. Ignatius,* trans. Anthony Mottola (Garden City: Image Books, 1964).

marked with familiar language, symbols, and categories. In this realm one knows by not knowing. One comes as close as possible to immediate perception of God. Teresa of Avila is an example of an apophatic contemplative. In her *Interior Castle,* she sketches the journey of the soul to the knowledge of God using the figure of traveling from the outer courtyard through seven stages to its most interior mansion. At each stage, the soul loses things that hinder its journey until, in the seventh house, the soul enters into spiritual marriage with God.[2]

While the contemplative tradition is stronger among Roman Catholics than Protestants, the Society of Friends is a community of Protestants who follow a form of contemplation. In the last generation an increasing number of garden variety Protestants have begun to practice contemplation. Such folk often say that recent Protestant piety is arid. They seek a living experience of the divine. Some Protestants today narrowly associate spirituality with contemplation. A few Protestants seek the experience of contemplation by turning to Eastern religions and other sources outside Christianity. The preacher can help such persons explore Christian patterns of contemplation.

Some persons who practice this tradition say they receive complete messages from God. Some of the mystics, for instance, report explicit images and verbal messages. Others report awarenesses that are less well defined but are still palpable, such as feelings leadings, and urges.

The great strength of contemplation is the sense of immediacy to the divine. However, sin so permeates the present world that it can corrupt even what appears to be a pure moment of contemplation. Every act of perception is an act of interpretation. Contemplatives can hear other voices (including their own) and attribute them to God. Consequently, contemplatives need to interpret their insights from the perspective of appropriateness to the gospel, intelligibility, and moral plausibility. Because this spirituality relies so much on personal revelation, a crucial component is to test the visions received through revelation in the community of faith.

## *The Common Life*

Many people today associate contemplation with spirituality and do not recognize that listening to God through tradition and the common life is an honored mode of spirituality. Although this

---

[2]Teresa of Avila, *The Interior Castle,* trans. Kiernan Kavanaugh and Otilio Rodriguez, The Classics of Western Spirituality (New York: Paulist Press, 1979).

approach is as old as the Bible, people often experience it as new when they discover it.

Interpreting the divine presence through sacred tradition and community assumes that God can be known through encounter with sacred tradition and the common life of the community. Persons who follow this path listen attentively for God's presence and leading through worship, the Bible, other texts that disclose the divine presence, and other aspects of community. The doctrine of the priesthood of all believers plays an important role, for this spirituality presumes that no one Christian possesses a full spectrum of understanding of the divine. The whole community is required to bring forth multiple gifts necessary for apprehending God and for supporting one another in responding faithfully to the gospel.

The Christian practices so frequently discussed in this book are fundamental to this approach to spirituality, especially listening attentively, worshiping God as a community, telling the Christian story to one another, interpreting the Bible and the history of the church's experience, as well as communal prayer.

The main service of worship is usually the center of this mode of spirituality. The ritual dramatizes God's relationship with the world and our response. We may distinguish four such spiritualities.[3]

1.  A spirituality centered in the union of word and table. The sermon and the breaking of the loaf are a sacramental unity that manifest and interpret the divine presence. This spirituality is now the official or semiofficial approach for Roman Catholics, the Orthodox, and many long-standing Protestant denominations. While many leaders officially commend this unity, some congregations in this stream lean toward a spirituality that is centered either in the table or in the word (categories 2 and 3).

2.  A spirituality centered in the table. In this approach, we become most fully attuned to God through receiving the bread and the cup. Although the Christian Church (Disciples of Christ), Christian Churches and Churches of Christ, Episcopal Church, and Roman Catholic Church subscribe to the union of word and table (category 1), many people in

---

[3]I adapt the first three categories from Carol M. Norén, "The Word of God in Worship: Preaching in Relationship to Liturgy," in *The Study of Liturgy,* ed. Chesslyn Jones, Geoffrey Wainwright and Edward Yarnold, rev. ed. (New York: Oxford University Press, 1992), 31–51. The fourth category is mine.

these churches are table centered. In some services of worship in the Christian Church (Disciples of Christ), the breaking of the loaf comes prior to the sermon. Some people partake of the sacrament and then leave the sanctuary before the sermon.

3. A spirituality centered in the word. This approach listens for the word of God through the Bible, the sermon, and other texts that help us become aware of the Holy. This spirituality is frequently found in congregations descended from the Anabaptists, and in community and Bible churches. It is also found among many congregations in denominations whose leaders recommend unity of word and sacrament, but whose weekly worship includes the sermon but not the sacred feast.

4. A spirituality centered in the experience of the Holy Spirit.[4] This approach apprehends God through the immediate movement of the Spirit in the service of worship, as well as in small-group or private devotion. Sometimes the experience of the Spirit is highly ecstatic and demonstrative, but it can also be quiet and almost contemplative. The Spirit often reveals the reign of God. Sometimes this spirituality results in the congregation's receiving direct messages from God. At other times, this spirituality results in experience of the divine presence but not a specific message.

Beyond the Sunday service, those who are oriented toward these four modes of spirituality often worship daily in the home or workplace. Daily devotions are more than private experience; they bring the power and vision of the worship of the main service into the home so as to freshen spiritual awareness. Worship in the home is a miniature of the major service. In full form, the daily practice of worship includes hymn singing, Bible reading, recitation of a creed or consideration of a thought from Christian theology, and prayer. This form is sometimes reduced to offering prayer before the meal and perhaps reading the Bible (or a devotional book) each day.[5] This spirituality often includes Bible study outside the Sunday service. The preacher can help the congregation recover the quickening power of daily worship.

---

[4]Steven J. Land, *Pentecostal Spirituality: A Passion for the Kingdom* (Sheffield, England: Sheffield Academic Press, 1993).

[5]For a contemporary resource for worship in the home, see Colbert S. Cartwright, "Daily Worship," in *Chalice Hymnal* (St. Louis: Chalice Press, 1995), 777–97.

A great strength of this spirituality is its communal character. Our spirituality is not dependent only on our individual awarenesses. The insights of the community supplement and correct the perceptions of individual Christians. The bodily feeling of the gathered community strengthens us; even when we worship at home alone, we are aware of being a part of a great cloud of witnesses.

Unfortunately, liturgy can become stagnant. Daily prayers can become *pro forma*. Communities can enshrine misperceptions of the Bible. Sin can distort the common life so that members do not adequately support one another. When such things occur, an important theme from the Reformed Movement helps: the church is to be reformed and always reforming. A part of the church's continuing quest is to find ways through which the church can become aware of the divine energy.

### Action in Life

While the "action in life" approach to spirituality seems new to many people today, it has been represented throughout Christian history.[6] It presumes that since God is active at all times and in all places, our sense of connection with God can be enhanced as we join the divine activity in the world. When a congregation becomes attuned to the movement of the Holy, members increase in both their immediate awareness of God and their capacity to apprehend God's larger purposes in the world. For instance, Parker Palmer says,

> Through action we both express and learn something of who we are, of the kind of world we have or want. Action, like a sacrament, is the visible form of an invisible spirit, an outward manifestation of an inward power. But as we act, we not only express what is in us and help give shape to the world; we also receive what is outside us, and we reshape our inner selves. When we act, the world acts back, and the world and we are co-created.[7]

Palmer, of course, emphasizes that action and reflection should inform each other. We need to reflect on the spiritual significance of our actions so that we can become as conscious as possible of the spiritual empowerment of the life of action.

---

[6]Janet W. Parachin, *Engaged Spirituality: Ten Lives of Contemplation and Action* (St. Louis: Chalice Press, 1999).

[7]Parker Palmer, *The Active Life: The Spirituality of Work, Creativity, and Caring* (San Francisco: Harper and Row, 1990), 17.

The church does not always recognize that engaging life in relationship with God can be a form of spirituality. However, persons for whom life-action spirituality is native find that it leaves them charged with awareness of the divine in the same way that a month of solitude leaves the contemplative. Action is how they relate to the world. Action is not utilitarian; it is a mode of perception and expression. Janet Parachin, who teaches at Phillips Theological Seminary, notes that many such people do not find a place in the church because they do not feel welcome in congregations whose spirituality is more contemplative or centered in sacred tradition and common life. Persons with a life-action spirituality sometimes receive messages that they are "not spiritual enough" from persons with other spiritualities.[8]

In this spirituality, action-oriented Christian practices are means of spirituality: carrying out service and witness, working together to maintain social structures that sustain life, struggling together to interpret the many interlocking contexts in which the congregation lives, and criticizing and resisting the principalities and powers.

Of course, persons who follow this spirituality must be able to distinguish God's presence and work from other force fields, values, and activities. This guidance typically comes through the practices of worship, telling the Christian story to one another, and interpreting the Bible. Through these means, congregations learn to recognize movements in history that are appropriate to the gospel, intelligible, and morally plausible.

We find this spirituality in many sectors of the church. For instance, many communities in the liberation movement manifest this form of spirituality. Such communities identify events in history in which God is liberating human beings or nature.[9] As people join the struggle for liberation, they become aware that they are joining God in a struggle in which God is already active; consequently, their own capacity for struggle increases.

This spirituality is frequently found among Christians who are deeply involved in social witness, such as staffing a residence for the homeless or working with Bread for the World. My father-in-law is a prime example. A mechanical engineer who worked on a team that designed a part for a vehicle that landed on the moon, he worships every Sunday, teaches the Bible, and has held most positions of leadership in a congregation. He has been involved for many years

---

[8]Janet Parachin, personal correspondence.
[9]Not all liberation theologians or communities manifest this spirituality.

in building houses through Habitat for Humanity. He told me that he feels closest to God and to the community when he spends the day, hammer in hand, working with other Christians. Even when he is physically drained at the end of the day, he is spiritually renewed.

Of course, one need not be engaged in a specifically Christian project for this spirituality to operate. Since God is omnipresent, this spirituality can nurture the self during any action in life. The preacher can help the congregation recognize that their nonchurch activities can feed them spiritually. From this perspective, visiting a sick neighbor or working at a food bank can be a time of spiritual regeneration.

A danger of this form of spirituality is that the people can become so active that they do not reflect sufficiently on the degree to which their activities are appropriate to the gospel, intelligible, and morally plausible. People who are spiritually immature or troubled can use busyness to escape confronting points at which they need theological clarification and even repentance. When activity becomes an end in itself, spirituality is subverted. Of course, as already noted, people with an engaged spirituality do need to reflect on the spiritual significance of their actions.[10]

### *Every Spirituality Should Bear Fruit in Life*

All the modes of spirituality described in this chapter presume that they will result in a life that testifies to the gospel. Indeed, one of the tests of the depth of the spirituality of a person or community is the degree to which the spirituality empowers that individual or congregation to witness in the world to God's unconditional love for all and God's will for justice for all.

This awareness is illustrated by a famous passage from the contemplative Thomas Merton, who describes stepping into a street filled with shoppers in downtown Louisville, Kentucky (near the monastery where he lived). He was filled "with the realization that they were mine and I theirs, that we could not be alien to one another, even though we were total strangers. It was like waking from a dream of separateness, of spurious self-isolation in a special world, the world of renunciation and supposed holiness. The whole illusion of a separate holy existence is a dream."[11]

From a systemic point of view, spirituality helps shape the identity and character of the congregation. This identity is embodied through

---

[10]See Parachin, *Engaged Spirituality.*

[11]Thomas Merton, *Conjectures of a Guilty Bystander* (New York: Doubleday Image Books, 1966), 158.

the congregation's actions within its own life and its actions in the wider world. These actions then cycle into the congregation's understanding of itself and its practice of spirituality. The practice of intercessory prayer, for instance, helps a group in the congregation be conscious of the needs of the world. Working in a food bank makes the group more aware of the needs of others. The group's practice of intercessory prayer in behalf of the hungry is then intensified, and they realize that a part of the Christian mission is to work for an economic system that makes food in abundance possible for all.[12]

## Spirituality and Preaching

The type of spirituality that permeates a congregation contributes powerfully to the character and shape of the congregational system. A contemplative spirituality tends to create a contemplative community. A word- and- table spirituality tends to create a community whose life flows from and toward table and pulpit. A life-action spirituality tends to create an active congregation.

Because spirituality embraces the whole of Christian life, preaching is not distinct from spirituality but is a strand in the whole fabric of spirituality. On the one hand, preaching helps shape and nurture the spirituality of the congregation. On the other hand, the spirituality of the congregation helps shape and nurture preaching. Preaching should help the congregation monitor the interplay between its spirituality and the actual functioning of its life system.

All persons and communities have their optimum modes of spirituality. The preacher needs to help persons and communities name their basic spiritualities so that they can nourish the forms of piety that are most beneficial and not become frustrated by trying to practice patterns that are alien. For instance, when I was a young adult, I tried to become contemplative. Despite repeated attempts and coaching, I could never satisfactorily quiet myself. My mind inevitably wandered. I felt guilty and spiritually incomplete. Hence, I was immensely relieved in seminary to discover that my lifelong habits of becoming aware of God by worship, daily Bible reading, and prayer are at the heart of an authentic tradition of spirituality. To be sure, I needed to enhance my practice of that tradition, but the tradition itself is not deficient.

I speak loosely of the congregation's having a mode of spirituality. However, today's congregations are composed of many different kinds

---

[12]See further, Palmer, *The Active Life*, 17–21.

of people. The typical congregation contains some people from all three basic types of spirituality. A preacher needs to help a congregation identify and nurture its dominant mode of spirituality while recognizing other forms of spirituality and the contributions those forms can make to the life of the congregation. The preacher can describe the basic approaches to spirituality, their benefits, and ways the congregation can practice them.

Preaching can nurture each type of spirituality in a slightly different way. However, each approach to preaching is based on the Christian practice of listening attentively and interpreting the divine presence. North Americans are so bombarded through the media with words, images, and music that many of us are sensorially numb. We do not attend sensitively to what happens around us. Yet words, music, and pictures often affect us unconsciously.

Consequently, the preacher can help most congregations by providing guidance in how to listen to the depths of the world. One of the most important skills in listening is to be able to describe what we hear, see, touch, taste, smell, feel, and think. We often need to learn to look beyond the meaning of such things on the surface to deeper concerns they represent. We can then interpret these phenomena from the standpoint of the gospel, and consider how the Christian community should relate to them.

An important contribution that preaching can make to spirituality is to introduce the congregation to skills that enable persons to listen attentively, to interpret what they hear from the perspective of the gospel, and to consider how what they hear contributes to (or frustrates) spirituality. The preacher can help the congregation identify ways they are affected consciously and unconsciously by the messages they receive.

We cannot name, in conventional language, all aspects of our experience of the divine. Bernard Meland, a theologian and philosopher, says that there "are depths of awareness accompanying the bodily event of living and experience that yield contributions to knowing which language may not convey, or, for that matter, cannot convey."[13] Meland continues, "*Presence*, sheer presence in and of itself is a mode of communicating."[14] Consequently, "Sheer appreciative awareness of that depth of existing is a gain in stature as a human being."[15] Contemplatives, for instance, cannot always fully articulate

---

[13]Bernard Meland, *Fallible Forms and Symbols* (Philadelphia: Fortress Press, 1976), 35.

[14]Ibid., 30. Meland's emphasis.

[15]Ibid.

the spiritual awareness that comes to them through contemplation. However, the preacher needs to help contemplatives push as far as possible toward conventional conceptuality to try to determine which awarenesses are appropriate to the gospel, intelligible, and morally plausible.

Systemically, preaching that helps the congregation listen more attentively to God present in the world also increases the capacity of members of the congregation to listen attentively to the sermon.

## Preaching and the Inner Life

Interpreting the divine presence and leading through the inner life often takes place in solitude or in settings that are silent. Even when contemplation occurs in corporate settings, preaching does not play the central role in contemplative spirituality that it does in some other modes of spiritual life. Nonetheless, sermons can nurture contemplative spirituality by helping acquaint the congregation with the practice of contemplation. The preacher can provide basic information. What is contemplation? How does it take place? What happens? What do we do with the content that emerges?

The most important contribution of preaching to this spirituality is to help the congregation form a theological ethos in which to contemplate by helping the congregation recognize (and critique) the kinds of knowledge of God that come through contemplation. Kay Bessler Northcutt, a Protestant contemplative, describes her work as preacher as helping the congregation shape its inner landscape.[16] The sermon helps populate the inner world with stories, principles, doctrines, images, and theological criteria that help contemplatives make Christian sense of the things that come to them.

I have heard several sermons with a contemplative quality from preachers who follow a spirituality of listening to God through the inner life. The preacher describes the content of an event of contemplation in such a way that the congregation imaginatively experiences the event. The preacher then helps the congregation reflect on how the contemplation adds to the life of the community.

The preacher can call attention to opportunities for contemplation within the service of worship. My denomination, the Christian Church (Disciples of Christ), observes the breaking of the loaf in a simple way each Sunday. The preacher can help the congregation recognize that the silence of that part of the service is ripe for contemplation.

---

[16]E.g., Kay Bessler Northcutt, *Praying by Heart: Prayers for Personal Devotion and Public Worship* (Cleveland: United Church Press, 1998).

The sermon itself can become an object of contemplation. The congregation may contemplate the way in which the preacher has broken open the gospel for the community.

The preacher can alert the congregation to situations outside the immediate life of the community that are ripe for contemplation, such as an event in the news, a phenomenon in nature, a local development.

I have also heard sermons, given in congregations in long-established Protestant denominations, that were designed to lead the congregation into contemplation, but that failed. In one memorable case, the preacher invited the congregation into contemplation during the sermon by calling for several minutes of silence in which the congregation was to meditate on the subject of the sermon. However, this congregation normally practiced a spirituality of listening to God through sacred tradition and common life. They did not possess the native orientation to enter into contemplation. As the silence lengthened, the sanctuary became restless, uneasy, and painful. Even congregations that contain large numbers of contemplatives cannot usually contemplate on command.

The sermon is seldom the time to invite the congregation into direct contemplation. Contemplation in worship normally takes place during prayer, around the breaking of the loaf, during the prelude or offertory music, during the anthem and the reading of scripture. In contemplative spirituality, a purpose of the sermon is to engage the community in conversation about the meaning of contemplation and about visions and other apprehensions that come to members of the community during contemplation. Sensitive worship leaders can leave moments of silence in the service when contemplation and reflection can occur.

The preacher needs to listen attentively to members of the congregation to ascertain the content of their contemplations. Persons listening to God through the inner life can forget that all human awareness is interpretive, and that contemplatives can misperceive the divine. Indeed, contemplatives can mistake their own wishes for the voice of God. Conversation through the sermon can help correct such imbalances. Sermons can help a congregation relate their spiritual apprehensions to the Bible and Christian tradition, evaluate them, and draw out the implications.

## Preaching and the Common Life

Preaching is an important part of the spirituality of interpreting the divine presence and leading through sacred tradition and the practices of the common life. Preaching, along with other components in the life system of the congregation, should perform an educational function of helping the community identify this form of spirituality and its practice. Many congregations in this spiritual tradition are theologically illiterate. They need basic information about this approach.

The preacher helps the congregation interpret the divine presence and leading. Preacher and congregation draw on key Christian practices–telling the Christian story, interpreting the Bible and the history of the church's experience, struggling to interpret the interlocking worlds of the congregation, criticizing the principalities and powers. A sermon can further become an experience of God with us. The sermon also helps the community discern God's presence and leading in the world beyond the church.

Sermons have particular nuances in each of the four spiritualities that are centered in listening to God through sacred tradition and the practices of the common life.

## WORD AND TABLE

A major task of the preacher in the spirituality centered in the union of word and table is to help the congregation understand the relationship between word and table as centerpoint in the congregation's spirituality.

The relationship between word and table in this spirituality is revealed in my own life. As a lifelong member of the Christian Church (Disciples of Christ), I have always had a high view of preaching. Yet my view made a quantum move when I was a student in the College of the Bible at Phillips University. My home congregation sang "Break Thou the Bread of Life" at least once a month as we gathered around the Table.[17] I associated the "bread of life" with the sacred feast. However, Robert L. Simpson, a systematic theologian, pointed out that in the hymn, the expression "bread of life" refers to the Bible and preaching. The practice of the church enlarged the meaning of the hymn to include the sacred supper. As Professor Simpson spoke, I recognized in my own experience the sacramental quality of preaching and the many times that the sermon is a means of grace. At the same time, I recognized that, as Augustine says, the sacrament

---

[17]Mary Lathbury and Alexander Groves, "Break Thou the Bread of Life," in *Chalice Hymnal* (St. Louis: Chalice Press, 1995), 321.

is a "visible word."[18] Preaching helps make that word explicit. Preaching and the breaking of the bread are different means through which the same gospel takes form in the heart of the community.[19] Together, word and table are a vital center of spirituality.

## TABLE AND WORD

Congregations whose basic spirituality is centered in the table sometimes have a limited view of preaching. For instance, in my class "Introduction to Preaching," Episcopalian and Roman Catholic students nearly always make gently self-deprecating remarks about preaching in their traditions. An Episcopalian student said, "The homily is usually only ten minutes. What can you do in ten minutes?"

I reply that a sermon can do a lot when it is clearly focused, brings the gospel into conversation with the deep concerns of life, and is embodied in a lively fashion. Such students are sometimes surprised to learn that preaching is undergoing a major renaissance in the Episcopal and Roman Catholic churches. Indeed, some of the most creative pulpit voices in the past and present belong to these churches (e.g., Phillips Brooks, Barbara Brown Taylor, Walter Burghardt, and Dorothy Day).

The preacher in the "table and word" community needs to help the congregation enlarge its expectation of the sermon. The preacher can do so by explaining what happens in preaching. Even more importantly, the pastor needs to preach in such a way that people recognize the important spiritual encounter that can take place through the pulpit. The preacher should not simply talk about spirituality but should preach so that the sermon can become an event through which the congregation encounters God.

The preacher further needs to help the congregation understand the feast. How is God present through bread and wine? What happens when we partake? At one level, of course, the preacher needs to help the congregation experience the supper as an assurance of God's unconditional love. The bread and the cup speak to us at the deepest dimensions of the self. At another level, the preacher can help the congregation realize that the supper of the Lamb is implicitly an ethical norm for the community. The love that God shows for all who eat

---

[18]Saint Augustine, *Tractates on the Gospel of John 55-111*, trans. John W. Rettig, The Fathers of the Church: A New Translation, vols. 90, 80.3, 117 (Washington, D.C.: The Catholic University of America, 1994).

[19]See further, *Breaking the Word: Essays on the Liturgical Dimensions of Preaching*, ed. Carl P. Daw, Jr. (New York: Church Hymnal Corporation, 1994).

and drink is paradigmatic of the love of God for all. In churches that receive all people at the table, that welcome represents the divine will for justice, for all persons to live in right relationship. Those who partake commit themselves to responding to the divine love by showing unconditional love for all and by witnessing to justice.

At the same time, the preacher needs to remember that the sermon is more than a communion meditation. The sermon needs to help the congregation interpret the whole of life from the perspective of the gospel, though with a special interest in how the breaking of the loaf helps us understand the divine presence and purposes in all circumstances. The sacrament of the table is a lens through which to perceive God's sacramental presence beyond the sanctuary.

## BIBLE AND WORD

Preaching in the tradition of listening to God through the word should clarify what is meant by the "word." This tradition centers on interpreting God's address to the world by means of the Bible. The "word," of course, includes more than the Bible. It includes the gospel and other modes by which God is present and active. The preacher needs to work with other elements in the congregational life system so that the community can become familiar with the foundational stories, characters, promises, commands, and principles of the Bible. This task is imperative in congregations that are biblically illiterate. A Christian community that does not know the Bible cannot satisfactorily practice any form of spirituality.

At another level, the preacher needs to help the congregation understand the nature of the Bible itself. How did it come to be? Who are the voices that speak in it? Whose voices are silenced, and why? One of the most important discoveries of biblical scholarship in recent centuries is the plurality of witnesses in the Bible, such as priestly, Deuteronomic, wisdom, apocalyptic, the various voices of the writers of the Second Testament. How do these different voices compare and contrast? And how do we mediate among them as to which are more or less reliable guides in helping us ascertain God's movement? Some texts in the Bible seem theologically or morally problematic. What role do such texts play in a spirituality centered in listening to the word? What do contemporary folk think, feel, and do when confronting situations for which the Bible has no direct address? Most importantly, how does conversation with the Bible help us become aware of God's presence and purposes?

The preacher may need to help the community understand that divine omnipresence means that God speaks through voices beyond the Bible. The preacher needs to help the congregation learn these voices and how they contribute to spiritual experience. The preacher also needs to help the congregation learn to recognize reliable contemporary interpreters, as well as false prophets.

This spirituality prompts us to recognize that God can be known through voices and means beyond the Christian tradition. Something of God can be known through non-Christians. We can encounter the divine presence and purposes through nature. If God is truly omnipresent, something of the divine may even be revealed through persons and communities who consciously distance themselves from the God of Israel.

At its height, the sermon transcends providing information about the voices of God. It becomes an occasion through which the divine presence becomes manifest in the community. Some people call this performative language. Another way of saying the same thing is to say that the sermon becomes sacrament.

Some churches that practice word-centered spirituality devalue the breaking of the loaf. Some such congregations spread the sacred table only quarterly, or less. I know a congregation that has the supper only after the Sunday evening service has been dismissed. Preachers in this tradition are called to help the congregation recover the sacred meal as a vital element in spiritual experience.

The spirituality of interpreting God through voices in the Bible, Christian tradition, and beyond is beset by an ongoing difficulty. Given the plurality of voices in these sources, which ones do we trust to lead us to God? The preacher must listen attentively to each voice so as to be able to commend voices that are appropriate to the gospel, intelligible, and morally plausible.

## HOLY SPIRIT

Preaching in the spirituality that is centered in the experience of the Holy Spirit must explain the nature and work of the Holy Spirit. What is the Spirit? How does it manifest itself? How do we receive it? The preacher can help the congregation understand what to expect when the Spirit breaks forth in worship or in small-group or personal settings. How does the knowledge of the presence of the Holy Spirit shape thoughts, feelings, and behavior in life beyond the congregation?

The sermon should help the congregation identify criteria by which to judge the degree to which the Spirit is present through particular phenomena and leading. Although the Spirit is often manifest ecstatically in the Bible and Christian tradition, the simple fact of ecstasy does not guarantee that the Spirit is at work. In the

Bible and Christian tradition, a frequent indicator of the presence of the Holy Spirit is the degree to which it helps the community enlarge its understanding of God's work in the world. In the Book of Acts, for instance, the Holy Spirit leads the early church to enlarge its understanding of the divine love by recognizing that God loves Gentiles and seeks to restore the broken relationship between Jewish and Gentile peoples. Again, the criteria of appropriateness to the gospel, intelligibility, and moral plausibility can assist the preacher and congregation in determining the direction of the leading of the Spirit.

## *Preaching and Action in Life*

Kay Bessler Northcutt, who leads spiritual life groups throughout North America, believes that a plurality of Christians in the United States have spirituality of action in life.[20] Persons in this mode of spirituality tend to be most receptive when they are bodily engaged in action. However, the sermon is important in life-action spirituality. The most basic contribution that the sermon can make to this spirituality is to help the congregation name listening to God through action in life as an authentic spirituality. Naming this approach as a legitimate form of spirituality can encourage people to practice it fully. People who have a life-action spirituality sometimes feel spiritually second-class. Furthermore, identifying this spirituality can enable people who follow its path to do so more conscientiously. When they view their activity as spiritual practice, their sense of connection with God can increase.

Another important contribution that preaching can make to persons in this approach is to help them form a theological consciousness that can function like radar, helping them recognize the divine presence in their engagement with the world. In order to interpret their actions theologically, persons with a life-action spirituality need an awareness of the overarching stories of the Bible, foundational Christian doctrines, and other resources necessary to make Christian sense of their actions. When they enter a life situation, they need to be able to sense God's presence and movement, and to join it. They need to know how God works in the world and how they can participate with God in the divine work. The sermon can join other parts of the congregational system in helping such people become acquainted with essential aspects of the Bible, Christian history and doctrine, and ethical norms.

---

[20]Kay Bessler Northcutt, personal correspondence.

Preaching can also provide moments of reflection when members of this spiritual group can name what they experience with God through their action in the world. What can they do to enhance the benefits of their spirituality? Are aspects of their activity getting in the way of their awareness of God?

Although the sermon is not an action in the same way as swinging a hammer while building a house with Habitat for Humanity, the preacher can sometimes feed people of this spiritual stream by describing an action through which participants draw closer to God. The congregation feels the action by means of the imagination.[21]

However, a preacher should invite the congregation to participate in actions during the sermon only when the congregation is adequately prepared. I recall a preacher trying to get the congregation to perform an action during a sermon that helped teach me this lesson. It was Maundy Thursday in a small congregation that did not regularly practice foot washing. The sermon was based on the story in John 13 of Jesus washing the disciples' feet. As a part of the sermon, the pastor asked the community to wash one another's feet. Water and basin appeared. People fumbled. They did not have a clear idea of the mechanics of foot washing. Several of the women were wearing hosiery that they could not remove. A few people were very uncomfortable with the idea of having their feet touched. At least two people were embarrassed because their feet were dirty. The people tried to wash one another's feet while sitting and moving in the cramped space between the pews. The experience was very awkward. After the foot washing, the sermon continued, but the congregation was disoriented. The action got in the way of the spiritual encounter that it was supposed to encourage. Such events require both an appropriate setting and adequate preparation for the congregation.

On the one hand, the preacher can help persons with a life-action spirituality envision the degree to which actions show promise of helping participants find fullness of Christian experience. Indeed, the preacher can help the congregation recognize points at which life-action spirituality helps the congregation enlarge its vision of God and the divine purposes in the world. On the other hand, the preacher can help such persons recognize ways in which actions in the world

---

[21]Pamela Moeller proposes a "kinesthetic homiletic," that is, an approach to the preparation of the sermon that takes advantage of the knowledge in the body itself, in her *A Kinesthetic Homiletic: Embodying the Gospel* (Minneapolis: Fortress Press, 1993).

sometimes work against apprehending the divine presence and purposes.

## Preaching and Spiritual Honesty

One of the most important services preachers can render to the congregation is to be honest about their own spiritual lives. Many lay people think that spiritual life should take place on a persistent high plane. They are disappointed when their spiritual awareness has peaks and valleys. However, dry periods of spirituality come to all people, including clergy, even those who faithfully perform Christian practices. The preacher can help the congregation understand that ebb and flow is a part of normal spirituality.

Sermons can celebrate the high moments when spiritual awareness flows through the pastor like electricity. Sermons can also help the congregation deal with seasons when spiritual voltage is low. Such sermons can relieve members of the congregation by assuring them that their own highs and lows are a normal part of the spiritual life. Such a sermon can also encourage the community to continue in its Christian practices in the certainty that such practice will help the community make its way out of an empty spiritual valley, or manage the electricity that charges self and community. Furthermore, honesty in the sermon increases the bond between preacher and congregation as people identify with the preacher as human being.

## Vital Spiritual Life

A key to spiritual preaching is for the preacher to have a vital spiritual life. In order to have vital spiritual lives, preachers must identify their optimum modes of spirituality and engage in practices that are characteristic of those spiritualities.

One approach to spiritual life does not fit all ministers. Pastors must find patterns of practice that are congenial with their spiritualities and with their lifestyles. Preachers need to engage in spiritual practices at times and places when they are most receptive to spiritual insights.

Preachers with a spirituality of interpreting the divine presence and leading through the inner life need to make the time to practice contemplation. Some people can keep attuned by entering into silence for fifteen minutes or an hour a day while others require regular periods of extended contemplation, such as a week, a month, or longer. Some preachers require spiritual directors or guides who can help structure and process the preacher's contemplations. One of my colleagues with a contemplative spirituality goes regularly to a

Carmelite monastery near the seminary for individual seasons of prayer and to join in the contemplative worship of the Carmelite sisters.

Preachers with a spirituality of interpreting the divine presence and leading through sacred tradition and the practices of the common life need to find time to engage in the Christian practice of corporate worship and attending to the Bible and other texts with disclosive power. In addition to participating in worship each week, some ministers need to put a devotional time on their calendars each day. I know preachers who set aside the first thirty minutes of every morning for Bible reading, prayer, and meditation. Others are most attentive to God late at night. Still others maintain their spirituality by taking two-day retreats for Bible reading and prayer every month or six weeks. Preachers sometimes try to get such retreats to do double duty by providing clergy with opportunities to plan sermons for a season of the Christian year, or even for a calendar year. However, it is easy for such a double-duty retreat to become confused, with the business of outlining sermons preempting spiritual renewal. Most preachers are well served by taking two distinct retreats: one for spiritual regeneration and the other for sermon planning. The two will still feed each other.

I do not require a quiet, removed time to maintain a piety in this vein. My spirituality is refreshed through participation in worship in our congregation and at the seminary, through Bible study classes that I attend in our congregation and that I teach at the seminary, and through prayer as I ride the exercise bicycle each day.

One of my most generative spiritual activities is reading books of Christian history and theology. Writing every day (as on this book) is also a spiritual discipline for me.

Since I not only teach Second Testament and homiletics but also preach, seminary students often ask, "How do you read the Bible devotionally in contrast to your critical, scholarly investigation of it?" I respond that my experience is that these two activities are not in conflict. I regard the Bible not as an inert object on which I perform surgical-like scholarly procedures, but as a genuine Other with its own integrity, life, and witnesses.[22] Regardless of the circumstances under which we encounter it, we seek to hear its word and to engage in conversation with it, and with others from tradition and contemporary life, to help the church discern God's continuing presence and purposes.

---

[22]Clark M. Williamson and Ronald J. Allen, *Adventures of the Spirit: A Guide to Worship from the Perspective of Process Theology* (Lanham: University Press of America, 1987), 115–35; Ronald J. Allen, "Preaching and the Other," *Worship* (forthcoming).

The intent of scholarly investigation is to help the church hear the Bible as much as possible in the Bible's own voices and not simply to project our own desires and values into the Bible. Scholarship is a friend who aims to discipline and focus our conversation with the text. Frequently, an activity like counting the number of Greek words in a passage turns into a luminous moment of spiritual insight in my study. A student's in-class report on an aspect of technical biblical criticism can spark a discussion of existential depth.

To be utterly candid, I think that many pastors who speak of a "devotional" reading of the Bible in contrast to "scholarly" interpretation do not have an adequate grasp of biblical scholarship in the service of the gospel and are not willing to take the time to explore this relationship. Some pastors seek to hear from the Bible only what they want to hear. Frequently, they project onto the Bible their own thoughts, feelings, and behaviors, and give the Bible no opportunity to speak a word that could enlarge, deepen, challenge, or correct.

Preachers with a spirituality of interpreting the divine presence and leading through action in life need to find opportunities through which to engage in actions that feed the self. I noted earlier that many people working in ministries of social justice are oriented toward this spirituality. A vigil outside a judge's chambers can be a prayer meeting to such folk. I know several pastors in this spiritual stream for whom a worktrip to another country is spiritually regenerative. A friend, an extrovert with a life-action spirituality and a pastor in a small town in western Missouri, finds soul rejuvenation by interacting with townspeople in the afternoon at the coffee shop. Some pastors with a kinesthetic spirituality come alive spiritually when they engage in body movement either individually or as part of a group.

Although preachers need to practice their particular spiritualities, they need to be careful not to make idols of their own approaches. When we find a spirituality that works for us, we sometimes assume that it should be normative for everyone. We can forget that the plurality of kinds of people in the church and world calls for pluriform spirituality.

Because the preacher represents the congregation, the preacher needs to be aware of modes of spirituality other than those that the preacher prefers and to be able to help people practice those modes. As mentioned earlier in this chapter, Janet Parachin noted that some congregations inadvertently turn off some people by leaving the impression that only one form of spirituality is normative. People who do not fit that spiritual mold feel out of place, perhaps even sub-Christian. They drift away from church.

Members of the congregation whose spiritualities are healthier than that of the pastor sometimes intimidate a pastor. Such pastors are tempted not to expose their spirituality to the congregation for fear of being considered an inadequate spiritual leader. At such times, the minister can put the doctrine of the priesthood of all believers into action. Laity with a special spiritual sensitivity can often help guide the pastor toward a fuller spiritual life. Preachers who tell stories of being helped spiritually by members of the congregation model the priesthood of all believers. If pastors do not attend to their own spiritual atrophy, spiritual weakness will undermine their ministries.

Preachers sometimes encounter a conflict between being a worship leader (and preacher) and the need to be fed through the service of worship and preaching. The tension that accompanies worship leadership sometimes detracts from the preacher's own ability to worship. The minister can be so self-conscious about wanting to get the mechanics of the service right that all other thoughts and awarenesses are pushed from the mind. Some of my most profound spiritual experiences come while serving at the table or in the process of preparing sermons. However, ministers who never gain the ability to worship while leading worship can take advantage of the ecumenical nature of the church and worship with another congregation that has services at a time the pastor can attend. Indeed, such cross-pollination may fertilize the minister's own spirituality.

The preacher who maintains a vital spirituality frequently becomes increasingly aware of God present and moving throughout the life-system of the congregation. A perceptive spirituality enables the pastor to feel the divine presence in education, in pastoral care and counseling, in mission, and even in administration. Indeed, a spiritually alive preacher can feel God involved in the preparation of the sermon. Under these conditions, the work of ministry actually feeds the spirituality of the minister. Service in the name of the gospel becomes a means of grace.

## Implications for Preachers

Spirituality—ways in which human beings attempt to become attuned to the presence and purposes of God—is central to the life of the pastor and the congregation. Christian spirituality is expressed in three basic modes (through interpreting the divine presence through the inner life, through attending to sacred tradition and common life, through actions). Given the fact that the congregation is a system, everything that happens in the congregation can contribute to (or frustrate) the community's spirituality.

At one level, the sermon interprets the spirituality of the community. At another level, participating in the sermon is an act of spirituality. Indeed, for the pastor, sermon preparation can be a deeply spiritual experience. The sermon can guide and participate in the spiritual life of the congregation in multiple ways:

- Help the church learn or remember the purpose of spirituality and help the community recognize that this purpose is inherent to the broader purpose of the Christian life.

- Help the church discover or remember its particular mode of spirituality (through interpreting the divine presence through the inner life, through attending to sacred tradition and common life, through actions), and help the congregation identify the chief characteristics and practices associated with its mode of spirituality.

- Help the community realize that spirituality is not an isolated activity within the church but permeates all that the church is and does.

- Help the congregation reflect on the degree to which the community's practice of its spirituality is appropriate to the gospel, intelligible, and morally plausible.

- Be alert to ways in which the practice of the spirituality in the congregation (or the lack of such practice) suggests themes for preaching. For instance, do aspects of the community's spirituality raise questions that should be addressed?

- Help the congregation recognize that while a particular spirituality may predominate in a congregation, the community should honor and accommodate other forms.

- Help the congregation cultivate the Christian practices that encourage the congregation's spirituality. For instance, the preacher needs to help the congregation develop a prayer life.

- Help the congregation identify the fruit in everyday life that should be born of every spirituality, such as love for God and one another, and justice.

- Show how the preacher engages in the practices that are vital to the preacher's own mode of spirituality so that the preaching is fed by a living spirituality.

- Help the congregation name injustice within its own life, and point the way toward repentance and renewal.

- Help the congregation recognize the importance of honesty in all phases of a congregation's spirituality.

## Implications for Spirituality

Pastors often preach on only one spirituality (often being unconscious of this limitation). Leaders in spirituality could develop instruments that help preachers name their own spirituality. Leaders in spirituality could further help preachers by providing guidelines for preaching beyond one's own spirituality for the sake of members of the congregation whose spiritualities differ from that of the preacher. What can a contemplative do to help a person whose spirituality is attuned to sacred tradition and the common life or to life action?

Instruction in both spirituality and preaching tends to be generic with respect to the relationship between the two. Neither experts in spirituality nor preachers have given much attention to the qualities of preaching that are (or should be) characteristic of each mode of spirituality. Leaders in the field of spirituality could help preachers by describing the kinds of sermons that emanate from each approach and by providing illustrations of each.

Many pastors have difficulty maintaining their own spiritualities and would profit from retreats and other kinds of experiences in which they could nurture their own spiritualities. Even pastors who regularly practice their modes of spirituality in the congregations that they serve often benefit from leaving the congregation to engage in their spiritual practice. Leaders in spirituality can help pastors by providing occasions that nurture the three dominant modes of spiritual life. At present, contemplatives can usually find spiritual guides and retreat centers where they can practice the silence necessary to sustain spirituality. However, pastors whose spirituality is fed by attending to sacred tradition and the common life often have much more difficulty locating communities beyond the congregation in which they can exercise this form of spirituality. Such occasions are needed. Pastors whose spirituality is centered in life action need both to recognize that spirituality as spirituality and to have occasions in which they can put it into practice and interpret it. Many such pastors already participate in hands-on activities in the congregation and in mission projects beyond the congregation that nurture this kind of spirituality, but they typically need more opportunity for reflecting on the spirituality of these occasions.

## Suggestions for Further Reading

Maas, Robin, and Gabriel O'Donnel, eds. *Spiritual Traditions for the Contemporary Church.* Nashville: Abingdon Press, 1990. Useful typology of different approaches to spirituality.

McGinn, Bernard, and John Meyendorff. *Christian Spirituality.* 3 vols. New York: Crossroad, 1986, 1989. Comprehensive history of spirituality.

Palmer, Parker. *The Active Life: The Spirituality of Work, Creativity, and Caring.* San Francisco: Harper and Row, 1990. Encourages spiritual persons to hold together action and reflection.

Parachin, Janet W. *Engaged Spirituality: Ten Lives of Contemplation and Action.* St. Louis: Chalice Press, 1999. Ten spiritual autobiographies showing how engagement and spiritual reflection work together.

.

# Subject Index

## A

academic disciplines and preaching, 1–2, 26–27, 44–45, 68, 92–93, 117–18, 142

administration: see leadership

administrative renewal in today's world, 79–96

administrator, preacher as, 71–94

apophatic (negative) spirituality, 120–21

appropriateness to gospel, criterion of, 9–10

## B

body, congregation as, 5–6

## C

calling in home and workplace, and preaching, 58

charismatic leadership in community, 72–73

Christian education: see education, Christian

Christian education through congregational practice, 34–36

Christian education and preaching, 29–46
  formal programs of Christian education and preaching, 37–39
  informal elements of Christian education and preaching, 39–40

Christian practice forms congregation as community, 36–37

community of care, congregation as, 54–60

congregation as system, 5–28

contemporary patterns of understanding mission, 101–13
  postliberal, 101–2
  revisionary (public church), 102–3

conversation, preaching as, 17–18

counseling (see pastoral care)
  Christian practices, and, 59–60
  community provides, 54–57
  helps people respond to gospel, 58–59
  individual therapy as older model, 52–54

preaching, and, 62–66

curricula in the congregation (explicit, hidden, null), 40–41

## E

education, Christian
  attentive listening in, 42–43
  explicit curriculum, 40–41
  formal programs of, and preaching, 37–39
  forms congregation as community, 36–37
  functionalist approach to, 32–34
  hidden curriculum, 40
  in ancient church, 31–32
  in Israel and earliest church, 29–31
  in Reformation, 32
  informal Christian education and preaching, 39–40
  null curriculum, 40–41
  practice forms community, 36–38
  preaching
    curricula (explicit, hidden, null), and, 40–41
    formal programs of Christian education, and, 37–39
    informal Christian education, and, 39–40
    interprets Christian practices, 41–43
    practice as, in Christian education, 37–43
    program, Christian education as, 32–34, 37–39
    sermon interprets Christian practices, 41–43
    Sunday school, 32–33
    through congregational practice, 34–36

enlightenment, effect upon understanding mission, 100–101

evangelism as expression of mission, 105–8

exemplary practice, preaching as, 16–17

explicit curricula in congregation, 40–41

**F**

formal elements of congregational system, 21–22
functionalist approach to Christian education, 32–35

**H**

healing pastoral care, and preaching, 56–58, 61–62
hidden curricula in congregation, 40–41

**I**

implications
  administrative theory for preaching, 91–92
  Christian education for preaching, 43–44
  Christian practice for preaching, 25–26
  counseling for preaching, 66–67
  creating a Christian society, mission as, 98–100
  in–church preaching, 111–13
  leadership theory for preaching, 91–92
  missiology for preaching, 116–17
  preaching
    for administration, 92–93
    for Christian education, 44–45
    for counseling, 67–68
    for leadership theory, 92–93
    for missiology, 117–18
    for spirituality, 142
  spirituality for preaching, 140–41
  systems theory for preaching, 25–26
informal elements of congregational system, 22–23
intelligibility, criterion of 10–12
  believability, 11
  clarity, 10
  logical consistency, 10–11
  seriously imaginable, 11

**J**

justice, witness to as mission of church, 108–9

**K**

kataphatic (affirmative) spirituality, 120

**L**

leadership
  chaos and disorder as seedbed for, 81–82
  charismatic, 72–73
  Christian practice, and, 82–84
  communal models of, 76–78
  corporate model, 75–76
  expression of institutional authority, 72–73
  in Israel and early church, 72–73
  in the Reformation and beyond, 74–75
  laity, central role in administration, mission, 84–86
  learning organization, church as, 8–86
  managerial approach in church, 75–76
  new science providing clues for, 80–81
  Newtonian models of organization, 80–81
  preaching, and, 76–78, 86–90
  Reformation, 74–75
  renewal in today's world, 79–86
  synergism, 82–84
  teaching, central role of in leadership, 78–80
  vision, helping community achieve important in leadership, 78–79
learning organization, church as, 85–86
life as mission, 115–16
life system, congregation as, 5–28
love, pure unbounded as key to theology of mission, 103–5

**M**

mission,
  clear sense of importance of, 84–86
  contemporary patterns of, 101–3
  creating a Christian society as, 98–100
  Enlightenment, in, 100–101
  evangelism as, 105–8
  in–church preaching, 111–13
  Israel and early church, in, 96–98
  justice, witness to, as, 108–9

leadership and, 82–89
learning organization, church as,
   85–86
mission, life as, 115–16
out–church preaching, 111–13
persons who have no sense of
   transcendent, 105–8
postliberal approach to, 100–101
practices, Christian, and, 105,
   110–11
preaching as, 110–15
public church, 101–2
Reformation, in, 99–100
statements, mission, generated
   by congregations, 85–87
theology of, 103
witness to justice through
   preaching, 113–15
world religions and Christian
   mission, 105–8
vision, most important contribution of preaching to, 78
missionary, preacher as, 95–118
moral plausibility, criterion of, 12

**N**
new science and implications for
   administration and leadership,
   80–83
Newtonian model of administration, 80–81
null curricula in congregation, 40–44

**O**
out–church preaching, 111–13
overcoming theological amnesia in
   preaching as pastoral care, 62–63

**P**
pastor, preacher as, 47–70
pastoral care
   Christian practices, and, 59–60
   community formation as result
      of, 54–57
   congregation as community of,
      54–57
   counseling, as, 62–66
   formation of community, 52–53
   Gregory the Great, 49–50
   healing, 56–58
   helps people respond to gospel,
      58–59
   individual therapy, 52–53
   Israel and early church, 50–51
   pastoral calling, and, 58
   pastoral counseling and
      preaching, 62–66
      overcoming theological
         amnesia, 62–64
      taking account of social
         context, 64–66
      transcending individualistic
         understanding of self, 64
   practices, Christian, in, 59–60
   preaching, and, 47–70
      develops community of
         pastoral care, 60–62
      overcoming theological
         amnesia in pastoral counseling,
         62–64
      takes account of social context
         in pastoral counseling, 64–65
      transcends individualistic
         understanding of self, 64
   preventive, 55–56
   Reformation and following
      periods, 50–52
   shepherding as image of, 48–49
   world, congregation exercises
      pastoral care for, 66
practice, defined, 13–14
practice, Christian,
   administration and, 76–80, 86–90
   community of pastoral care,
      and, 60–62
   congregational system, and, 12–
      14, 24–25
   counseling and, 59–60, 62–66
   defined, 1–2, 12–17
   importance of, 16
   interrelationship of practices, 15–16
   leadership and, 76–80, 86–90
   mission and, 105, 110–11
   not all repeated activities are, 17–18
   preaching as, 16–17, 24–25
   representative list of thirteen
      practices, 14–15
   spiritual life and, 119–43
   synergism among Christian
      practices in leadership, 82–84
   system, and, 1–2, 12–17
   teaching and, 34–37

preaching
    administration and, 71–94
    affected by community, 19–20
    Christian practice, and, 16–18,
        24–25
    conversation, as, 18–19, 41–42
    counseling, as, 47–70
    exemplary testimony, as, 16–17
    formal, informal and tacit
        elements of congregational
        system, and, 21–24
    in–church, 111–13
    mission, as, 95–118
    out–church, 111–13
    part of life system of congregation,
        as, 1–2, 5–28
    representative, 16–17
    spiritual leadership, and, 119–43
    teaching, and, 29–46
    vital spiritual life, and, 137–40
    witness to justice, 113–15
preventive pastoral care and
    preaching, 56–57, 60–61

**R**

reign of God, mission as participat-
    ing in, 96–98

**S**

sermons: see preaching
shepherd as image for pastoral role,
    48–50
spiritual honesty in preaching, 137
spiritual leader, preacher as, 119–43
spiritual life, vital, 137–40
spirituality
    bear fruit in life, 126–27
    Christian practices and, 119,
        122–24, 125, 126–27, 128, 130,
        131, 133–34, 136, 137–40
    personal and corporate,
        relationship of, 120
    types of, 120–27
        action in life, 124–26, 129–30
        common life, 121–24, 130–35
            Holy Spirit, centered in
                experience of, 123, 134–35
            table, centered in, 122–23,
                131–32
            word and table, centered in,
                122, 133

word, centered in, 123, 133–34
    contemplation, 120–21
    inner life, 120–21
        apophatic (negative), 120–21
        kataphatic (affirmative), 120
    preaching, and, 127–37
        action in life, 135–37
        common life, 130–35
            Holy Spirit, experience of,
                134–35
            table, centered in, 131–32
            vital spiritual life, and, 137–40
            word and table, centered in,
                132–33
            word, centered in, 133–34
        inner life, spirituality of, and
            preaching 129–30
        spiritual honesty, and, 137
    vital spiritual life, 137–40
Sunday school, 32–34
synergism and Christian practice,
    82–84
system
    congregation as, 1–2, 8–9
    congregational practices, and,
        12–16
    defined, 6–8
    formal elements of congrega-
        tional, 21–22
    informal elements of congrega-
        tional, 22–23
    preaching in congregational, 18–21
    tacit elements of congregational,
        23–24

**T**

tacit elements of congregational
    system, 23
taking account of social context in
    preaching and pastoral care, 64–66
teacher, preacher as, 29–46
teaching, primary responsibility of
    pastor as administrator/leader,
    78–79
theological criteria, 9–12
    appropriateness to gospel, 9–10
    intelligibility, 10–12
    moral plausibility, 12
transcendence, preaching to persons
    who have no sense of, 105–8

transcending individualistic understanding of self in preaching as
  pastoral care, 64
types of spirituality, 120–27

**W**

witness to justice through preaching,
  113–15

world religions, Christian mission
  in relationship to, 105–8

**Z**

zero-based approach to church
  planning and organization, 81–82